WINNING THE LAND-USE GAME

A Guide for Developers and Citizen Protesters

Carolyn J. Logan

PRAEGER

PRAEGER SPECIAL STUDIES • PRAEGER SCIENTIFIC

Library of Congress Cataloging in Publication Data

Logan, Carolyn J.
    Winning the land-use game.

    Includes index.
    1. Land use—Planning—Citizen participation.
I. Title.
HD108.6.L63   333.73′17   81–15710
ISBN 0-03-059658-0   AACR2

Published in 1982 by Praeger Publishers
CBS Educational and Professional Publishing
a Division of CBS Inc.
521 Fifth Avenue, New York, New York 10175 U.S.A.

23456789   145   987654321

Printed in the United States of America

Dedicated to William "B. J." Johnston, whose journalism classes at the University of Washington have inspired countless students, including myself; and dedicated to my loved ones. Special gratitude goes to John Case.

CONTENTS

INTRODUCTION

Developers put the wheels in motion when they apply for a re-zone or building permit for construction of a new business or apartment building. But hostile homeowners fear tax increases and traffic jams; so they resist rezones, trying to still the spinning wheel. Then developers counterattack. The war worsens in the hearing room. The unschooled lose.

Knowledge, however, turns the victims into the victorious. This book equips both sides for a fair fight. It spells out some of their rights. To win the zoning game, developers and residents can arm themselves with an overview of the issues in Part I; with the nuts and bolts of success in Part II; and with ways to build for the future in Part III. The forerunner of this account of land-use practices also proved popular with architects, lawyers, and real-estate agents, for they commonly plead cases before hearing officials on behalf of clients. In addition, it is used by those associated with government and as a textbook in University of Washington planning courses.

Part I, Chapter 1, centers on the issues. One issue is private-property rights. Some protesters erode the developers' property rights, depriving them of full use of their land in some cases. On the other hand, development generates higher taxes, driving some residents from their homes. Why, they ask in this chapter, should people who have lived in an area for years bear the burden of higher tax bills they can't afford?

This book aims to help defuse the dynamite, that is, reduce the explosive tension between developers and residents. Both sides will find solutions in the "Nuts and Bolts" section, which contains case histories, illustrating formulas for success. Part II, Chapter 3, pauses briefly with humorous "Dear Protester" letters, since humor is a vital ingredient in any land-use campaign. Then citizen craftsmen explain how to build strong cases for hearing presentations. "Come, now, let us reason together" (Isaiah 1:18) is the theme of the last half of this chapter, which contains check lists for opponents who wish to work out a compromise pact. One way to defuse the dynamite is to examine how the experts side-step friction and how they search out the roots of friction. Land-use lawyer Jerry Hillis shares his insights in Chapter 4. Hillis, recognized as a premier expert at finding cracks in zoning codes, knows how to work harmoniously with hearing officials and shares that expertise.

When he examines the anatomy of friction, he denounces the county.
"The policy of elected officials is not being carried out," he charges.
"A lot of staff members run off, making recommendations, contrary
to county policy." Ideally, the staff county planners recommend for
or against a rezone, based on county policy established in the past
by elected officials.

Land-use players will save time, money, and trouble when they
read 50 tips in Chapter 5, all gleaned from the experts. For instance,
why not avoid the pitfall of collecting petitions twice? Why not avert
water drainage problems, thus averting outcries from protesters?
Why not avoid the disfranchisement suffered by a crowd of 900? Finally, why not discover the combination that cracks the Environmental
Impact Statement (EIS) code? Learning the combination lets you help
write the EIS, a report issued by government on traffic and other potential impact from certain apartment and other proposed projects.
EIS reports determine whether building permits are issued or denied.
Moving on, Chapter 5 presents a case history on how citizen Davids
toppled the Goliath of government. Thanks to them, government
couldn't get a building permit for a prison in their backyard. As
government moves into the development business, some private developers hop aboard the bandwagon—at a profit. For details on this
trend, turn to Chapter 6. Developers get the same kind of nuts-and-
bolts assistance in Chapter 7 as protesters received in Chapter 3.
Each chapter is must reading for the opposite side.

Throughout the book, methods are presented that can be dupli-
cated by other citizens, developers, and governments. The reforms
of Chapter 8 are no exception. The next chapter, in Part III, Building for the Future, zeroes in on how certain city halls and courts
engineer integrity. That is, they work for procedures and precedents that prevent pay-offs. In format, Chapter 10 concludes Part
III; in substance, it opens the door to tomorrow. Here, the trend
setters step center stage, telling of new building practices that beat
the energy crunch; of streamlining that untangles red tape; and of
siting practices that will win the skirmish with shrinking land supplies. Here, too, innovative builders steal the show with their
$12,840 homes and $112,000 savings in interest fees. The appen-
dixes contain several items of interest, including one that takes
the novice step by step, from the rezone application, right up to
the hearing. One step in the process may be an Environmental Impact Statement. Only raw recruits will fail to read the EIS appendix
before they march into battle. Only the ill-prepared will overlook
the EIS excerpts on the proposed Boeing Headquarters.

Unfortunately, the length of time—about four years—consumed
by dozens of Boeing hearings is not uncommon. For land-use disputes typically sap resources, leaving losers on all sides. Con-

frontation is costly for both camps. Various strategies, ideas, and reforms offered herein can head off confrontation. It is hoped that this book will help protesters and developers resolve their differences more productively. Ideally, an even match would strike a balance between both camps.

PART I

The Issues

1

THE PRICE OF PROGRESS

Homeowners, usually unschooled in land-use practices, find change perplexing. They get up in arms when notified of a rezone for an apartment or tavern, or upon learning that a builder wants to convert "their woods" into condos. Embittered at development that appears to be slipping into existence, residents begin to plot. All too often, they are rendered impotent by ignorance. And the developers? They're often the giants in the area of savvy. But some are beginners who lack savvy about procedures, regulations, zoning, and ways to resist rebel residents. Seeking help, they turn to the growing army of land-use consultants. Developers, like residents, have a lot at stake.

They clash over issues that touch their pocketbooks and their lifestyles. Put simply, residents fear apartments and businesses will clog streets, prey on property taxes, and bring an onslaught of development. They see the public good threatened by profiteers. Developers, though, believe they uphold the public good when they fulfill demands for housing. They fight against erosion of their own private-property rights. Both sides howl over the issue of who pays for development, or development generates the need for new sewers, streets, and services, to some degree. Neither side wants to pay the bill.

Outcry over these issues reaches the ears of government decision makers. One hearing official says he works to ensure due process, separating the wheat of evidence from the chaff, arriving at a decision for the public good. Another says the underlying test in deciding a case is whether it conforms to county plans and policies.* At times, it's not black and white, she says. For example, will the proposed multi-units overlooking the business center adhere to a policy of multi-units next to business centers, or will the ravine in between define the multi-units as not in proximity to business? In another example, should the county community plan (designating single-family zoning for the site) govern, or should the county comprehensive plan (designating multi-units)? Bruce Laing, examiner turned county councilman, said that when a case is not black and white, his job as zoning examiner and councilman is to decide which plans and policies apply.

TAXES AND TRAFFIC

A closer look, now, gives a fuller examination of the issues. Homeowners typically want to maintain the status quo to protect their homes—perhaps their biggest investment—and to keep their lives free of more taxes and traffic. They worry about property tax impact, knowing that when that vacant lot is converted for condos, the condo owner's tax bill will spiral. Then their tax bill will rise—and their tempers will rise when traffic proves troublesome.

One angry resident, Harlan Olson, protested when the addition of 700 units threatened his neighborhood. He declared, "It's already stop and go to and from work. Appalling!" His Renton neighbors leave at 6:30 A.M., instead of 7:30 A.M., to get to work on time. Overall, residents see the public good threatened by profiteers. Righteousness reigns.

But developers also wear the cloak of virtue. "We are fulfilling the public's need for housing," they argue. Indeed, vacancies are scarce; a job boom promises more pressure. So does the population boom. The 20-24 age group outnumbers the 40-44 age group by more than two to one; the 15-19 bumper crop is the second largest in size. Shelter shortages won't go away.

Nor will the clash over private-property rights go away. Developers buy or own land that is idle or under-used, and are eager to exercise creativity and coax that land into a development. They seek a rezone to use the full capacity of that private land, believing individual freedom is important in this country. Ideally, they feel, they can replace that substandard building on the site with better

---

*In city cases, city plans and policies would be considered. Throughout this book, the term "county" is interchangeable with the term "city."

ones. Ideally, developers say, they can build a certain number of units per acre, thus earning a fair profit. Then protesters hamstring the developers, complaining of too many units, and the irritated developers resist reduced use (such as dropping density to half as many units per acre). Worse, developers suffer from undue delay, knowing it drives their interest fee up and their profit margin down. Protesters persist: change the height, change the landscaping. The developers resist changing plans in midstream, knowing such changes drive architectural fees up.

"All those residents did was complain," declared land-use lawyer Jerry Hillis. "No one talks about the special session that the zoning examiner held to explain the process to them. No one talks about how the plans, both of the county and of the developer, were changed to their benefit."

Tom Rhinevault sums up resentment when he dubs protesters tennis shoes, as in "little old ladies in tennis shoes." He said his training "college," the Land Education Foundation Inc., instructs developers on how to handle hostile homeowners and hostile ordinances. Rhinevault isn't the only one who is hostile to homeowners. Robert Stead, a lawyer representing residents, confided that resentment came to a boil at a rezone hearing when the developer threatened "to wipe me out."

BRAWL OVER SPRAWL

Hopes for a balance between developers and residents may dim as conditions intensity. One condition is the rising tide of red tape that plagues both sides. Politics persists. Community land plans issue the stern warning, "No developers need apply." The housing crunch swallows up bigger bites of land. A shrinking land supply, escalating population, and spiraling housing costs are on a collision course, warned lawyers Richard Aramburu and Hillis. ("Developers better watch out when Aramburu has the case," is how courthouse insiders characterize this land-use lawyer.) King County, the home of Seattle, Washington, increases its population by about 240 persons per day and is reported to be one of the fastest-growing areas in the nation. Many states suffer from growing pains. Growth sharpens the swords in the battle between developers and residents. It is the firewater that intensifies the conflict among population, land supplies, and housing costs.

As the population explosion spreads toward undeveloped land, a backlash brews against progrowth forces. As a result, the Washington Environmental Council has laid the groundwork for a state initiative to limit growth. Limited natural resources can't withstand heavy growth pressure, a council leader reasoned.

The backlash has also hit the ballot box. Development foes have ousted a majority of the Issaquah City Council, dubbing the election the "Issaquah massacre." Chris Himes, a growth-management advocate, cleaned house in Redmond City Hall when she captured the mayor's post. Nearby, Maria Cain was elected to a Bellevue City Council seat—although she probably won't be able to put a lid on high-rises as residents almost did in San Francisco's narrowly defeated Proposition O. A limit on growth was an issue in Ginni Stevens' race for Snohomish County Council too. "I boycott busy freeways and the new shopping center," asserted Stevens, expressing the crusading spirit characteristic of players in the property-development controversy.

Crusaders clash. When the "County Group" attempted to muster political clout in King County Council races, developers almost exterminated these citizen proponents of "graceful growth" and farmland preservation. In a separate movement, farmland-preservation proponents pushed the county's $50 million farmland-preservation bond issue. Bonds, approved by the voters, will buy development rights to secure up to 15,000 acres for agricultural use—if, that is, the plan isn't killed in court by antipreservationists. Crusaders also clashed over housing displacement. This issue sharpened when the Displacement Coalition caused several builders to provide moderately priced housing to compensate for demolished

units that were cleared to make way for new structures. Terre
Harris of the master builders' group held out an olive branch to the
coalition backers when he asked if they could work in concert to
boost housing supply.

Growth was an issue in the gubernatorial contest. One Democrat pressed then Governor Dixy Lee Ray to define her position on
the management of growth. Some say the Democratic governor
straddled the fence when she urged agencies to consider farmland
preservation in decision making, while arguing that decisions on
preservation rest with local officials. On the Republican side was
John Spellman, the longtime county executive who had campaigned
for the farmland-preservation bond. Spellman won the election,
despite Republican rivals who faulted him for mismanagement of
growth in the county.

In the county, people were "voting" with their feet; several
communities wanted to flee the county. The theme in these campaigns (Federal Way incorporation and McMicken, Riverton,
Allentown, and south Burien annexation) was: "We want more local
control over land use, especially to preserve our single-family
communities against developers." Governor Spellman, then county
executive, accepted annexation and incorporation as a right of self-
determination. His blueprint for the future showed most of the
county incorporated, with the county government in the role of a
service wholesaler. (Former Governor Ray's progrowth blueprint
was evident when she appointed master builders' and trades council
leaders to the board that rules on annexation and incorporation.
Ray did not reappoint Ann Aagaard, farmland-preservation stalwart.)

Despite the exodus, the county exerted more controls to cope
with growth, igniting a backlash. To direct growth, the county
pushed a 1978 sewer plan. Residents, developers, and the county
engaged in a slugfest, resulting in adoption of "a compromise plan,"
according to County Councilman Gary Grant. To accommodate
growth, government wanted to expand sewer plants to handle up to
396,800 acres. Resident Leon Harris organized a protest, saying
authorities then turned to "alternatives" (scaling down territory,
encouraging septic-tank use). To put the brakes on sprawl, the
county reduced minimum lot sizes and promoted growth management, which may control sprawl by guiding growth into areas easily
serviced by streets and sewers. To manage growth, the county
wanted to "in-fill" lots (build on vacant lots) in settled communities,
thus discouraging growth in semideveloped areas; but critics lashed
back, saying that measure wouldn't work. Then community plans
and scattered moratoriums locked the door against traditional
development. Angry developers began to feel private-property
rights are an endangered species.

"Bureaucracies and arrogance hold our land in hostage. We'll work for protection of private-property rights," vowed Bill Boeing Jr., son of the Boeing Company founder. He financed the new Property Owners of Washington with about $10,000. Boeing's group joined a state-wide federation to combat "overregulation." Members of the newborn federation unfurled the flag of Americans who will bear political arms against perceived usurpation of land-owners' rights. One ally was the Western Environmental Trade Association (WETA), long at odds with environmentalists. WETA is regarded as a progrowth labor-business group. Still another consortium, known as Newcastle, sprang up. Members, including Burlington Northern and Daon Corporation, collected a $150,000 fund to fight county regulations. In this era of activism, even the board of realtors—historically, a sleeping giant—wakened to flex its political muscle. The board kicked off a voter-registration drive of some 3,000 members at its annual meetings and the president proclaimed a new era of political activism.

Then the financial cross fire erupted; Boeing's group attacked the county's cost-of-growth analysis and collected ammunition to be used in a rebuttal. Little wonder tension mounted. Only the names of citizen groups—like Backward Thrust (a reaction to the Forward Thrust park bond)—lent a wry touch of humor.

TAMING MEGALOPOLIS

Almost lost in this brawl over sprawl are the quiet voices that advance solutions for tomorrow. They want to right some wrongs. Hillis saw shortsightedness when the county initiated G-5 (one unit per five acres) zoning. He warned that the entire effort of the county planning staff was to cut down density (units per acre). At the same time, he said, a growing population consumes land at an unbelievable rate per household. Hillis asked how much effort was being made to encourage high density on land suitable for it, and what the most environmentally sensitive path was.

In rare agreement, Hillis (whose clients are mostly developers) and Richard Aramburu (who represents only protesters) called for "super-growth" zoning. It would apply only to certain areas and would replace the current practice by which developers build no more than a set number of units per acre. Instead, the developer would be required to fill super-growth acreage with the maximum number of units permitted—or be denied a building permit. One implication is that super-growth zoning may help defuse the dynamite, reducing the tension between developers and citizens.

New zonings and new solutions are essential at this moment, since Washington State is expected to grow by 1 million people every 10 years in the next few decades. "Washington State is one of the last frontiers in terms of growth," declared Roger Leed, a lawyer who specializes in environmental law. "We're where California and the East were 20 years ago. That's why we have confrontation." Lawyer Aramburu has contended that this time is a turning point. He warns that bad land use can depress the economy because a discontented labor pool will flee, triggering relocation by industry. In his view, the Northwest now has an edge over Chicago and other despoiled places, an edge that he wants the Northwest to keep.

GROWTH GENERATES JOBS: GROWTH DRAINS TAXES

Clearly, growth is laced with economic considerations. For example, at stake are the livelihoods of those involved in real estate, architecture, and unions, as well as the economic well-being of industry. To illustrate: one firm's health was not faring well in the face of growth. The expansion plan of this Green River industry may die on the drawing board if Puget Power's restrictions are too confining. This industry finds that new growth outstrips the power supply. On the credit side, growth breeds a bigger tax base; on the debit side, growth demands tax money for roads, schools, and services. There are two major ways to pay for growth: taxpayers can pick up the tab or developers can pay fees to offset the cost of roads and other new services. Traditionally, taxpayers have been picking up the tab. For this reason, said Governor Spellman, a veteran member of the National Association of Counties' Land Use Committee, "We must control sprawl. Taxpayers have been subsidizing rural development when their taxes have gone for roads, sewers and water facilities."

Where sewers go, development follows. Some residents forgo sewers in an attempt to lock the door against development. Developers use sewer lines as miners would use a vein of gold to intrude into an area. Stopping developers from doing so is difficult because of loopholes in procedures, and because of independence and expansionism of sewer districts, according to Jim Mawson, a seasoned citizen activist. Judicial ploys may not succeed. In a Maple Valley case, residents were defeated in court when they attempted to block formation of a utility local improvement district. They didn't want to pay an estimated $3,000 per lot assessment for ground they called home. Developers, however, fought in favor of the district. Sewers can shoot up assessments and property taxes. Sewers may even define property taxes, as discussed in Land and

the Pipe. This study of 25 years of land sales, authored by two
Harvard professors and one from the Massachusetts Institute of
Technology, found that sewers always double and sometimes triple
property value. Where value jumps, property taxes play follow
the leader.

However, the trend toward charging developers fees for
services may bring relief for future taxpayers. California and
some other states insist that developers help pay their way. In
Issaquah, Washington, a $1,000 tax on new homes was under con-
sideration. King County followed suit when it began to consider
charging developers for county park acquisition. Even the 1979
legislature took a step in this direction, passing a bill to excuse
farmers temporarily from assessments caused by developers.

Even Hillis favors taxing developers for public facilities; for
him, the main question is how much they should pay. In early 1979,
Snohomish County commissioners decided that the right amount was
a percentage for schools, roads, sewers, parks, and fire districts,
and they set ceilings. Developers could be charged a maximum of
$1,000 per single-family home for schools. The maximum per-
mitted per multiple-family unit was $350. Fees for fire districts
could not exceed $200 per single-family home or multiple-family
unit. But the powerhouses that continue to pack a punch are the
master builders' groups. Legally, they defeated the fee regulation.
Undaunted, Snohomish officials worked to nullify the builders'
court victory. Snohomish, however, exemplifies places across the
nation where battles over fees often end up in the courtroom.
Lawyer Fred Jacobsen, writing in the North Carolina Law Review,
examined methods in states where fees (impact taxes) have been
upheld. He advocated such impact taxes.

Developers argue against fees, saying they harm the consumer,
as well as pinch the pocket of developers. They contend that this
regulation creates an artificial market, in which narrowing the
supply drives up housing costs, hurting the elderly and newly mar-
ried. "It's your children and grandchildren who'll need housing,"
they argue.

On the other hand, fee proponents feel it's unjust to subsidize
development. The tab in a Virginia county was in excess of $1
million for costs generated by an 800-unit development, according
to an Urban Institute researcher's study, financed by the Ford
Foundation. If, however, 800 units were spread out in a sprawling
community, they would incur twice the road and utility costs of a
compact arrangement, according to a Real Estate Corporation
study, The Costs of Sprawl. Put simply, a short sewer pipe is less
expensive than one stretching a couple of miles between homes.

FOR LAND'S SAKES

In the following case, county taxpayers found growth knocking at their front door. They forked over 13 percent of road expenses; in addition, neighbors near a new development were billed for roads.

Homeowner Jolly Hibbits was one of them. Years ago, Hibbits had been divorced. She began searching for someone who shared her desire to live in the country. "I kept hoping I'd run into someone along the way who also wanted to live outside the city," she said. "Finally, I said, since I can't find someone, I'll do it myself." Hibbits searched for just the right place, driving on weekends through the area within a 25-mile radius of the city. Eventually, she selected a wooded Woodinville site to fulfill a dream of raising her children in the country. It took years of work to clear the land, to build a home. Then Hibbits' dream turned into a nightmare. Suddenly there were 100 mailboxes on her road, one of which held her bill for "the price of progress." The assessment bill came when the new homeowners nearby formed a road improvement district; Hibbits' share of $405,000 was $11,456, plus interest, payable over 15 years.

Hibbits' bill was about $200 per month for roads and doubled property taxes. This single mother couldn't afford it. Her salary as a biologist meant take-home pay of only $362 every two weeks. Development hurts. She lashed back, denouncing the county since it had permitted construction. "I'm so mad I'm about ready to chain-saw down the county sign!" she declared. She resented real-estate agents and builders who had expanded her community of 12 to 126. Builders shouldn't have been allowed in, unless they brought the roads up to standards, she said bitterly. People who are already here shouldn't have to shoulder the burden. Why, she asked, should people who lived here for years have to bear the burden of subsidizing development?

Angry, upset, Hibbits didn't know which way to turn. She desperately sought a solution. Maybe subdividing would pay off the $11,456. But she quickly dismissed the idea because her plot of land was too long and skinny to subdivide. Any profit, she felt, would be eaten up when she tried to buy another chunk of land at today's prices. Prices had escalated since she paid $27,000 for ten acres six years ago. Her search for a solution was exhausted. Her only recourse was a forced sale—and tears. The price of progress? How do you measure the emotional scars? "I've cleared my land, built my house. My heart and soul are here." Hibbits' heart and soul don't matter.

PART II
Nuts and Bolts

2

CLOUT THROUGH
COMMUNITY GROUPS

Years ago, neighbors knew one another. They pitched in with harvests and house raisings. Today, neighbors live isolated from one another until someone spots a rezone notice. Immediately, strangers become friends, forming informal groups for self-protection. Immediately, networking unfolds: "Let's ask Betty for help. She knows everyone up on the hill." Through networking, citizens swap ideas, pool expertise, divide up prehearing work, and mobilize many for the hearing. Novices learn from old hands who've been through zoning battles before. By reading this book, one can learn from old hands who fight against rezones and building permits.

The value of community groups extends beyond the everyday nuts and bolts, to a deeper value. These groups are democracy in action, an antidote to the administrative power of the growing army of staff members. They're the squeaky wheel that demands oil in the form of accountability from elected officials, who sometimes forget this country operates on a ballot-box system. Ideally, they're government watchdogs, making sure government doesn't overstep the bounds of zoning and subdivision authority.

Ideals, however, rarely materialize. True, an occasional group studies county land plans, gaining long-range responsiveness by providing input over the years. More often, homeowners fail to notice impending rezones until an apartment, tavern, or garbage landfill hits their backyard. Only then do they unite in ad hoc community groups—Spellman dubs them "Homeowners' Protection Societies." Too late and too weak is often the hearing verdict. Groups, discouraged, disband after the rezone fight. They may have worked at a disadvantage, for they're often outweighed by the developer's more sophisticated tools—local affiliations with real-estate boards and master builders, as well as with counterparts to the progrowth

Western Environmental Trade Council and the Land Use Research
Council (a pipeline of updates on zoning). Governor Spellman wants
to even the balance. He has long sought to strengthen community
councils that are representative. "We need community councils
with legal status," he urged. "They can observe rezones and land-
use changes, so a citizen doesn't have to flounder by himself every
time he suddenly sees a vacant lot looking like it's turning into a
gas station."

REZONE CONSEQUENCES

A lone citizen, looking at that vacant lot, can see what's at
stake with this thumbnail sketch. Rezones (and land-use changes
like subdivisions) can change school enrollment, the character of
the neighborhood, and the lifestyle of the occupants. But the sharp-
est consequence is tax impact. Rezones can have a ripple effect,
both on taxes and on use. Here's how it unfolds in a residential
neighborhood:* Traffic impacts and substantial change in the character of a neighborhood from the multiple-family project will make use
of adjoining property for single-family homes less attractive. Therefore, vacant lots will be rezoned and homes may be rezoned. As
more apartments are built, pressure is created for still more rezones and apartments. Services and improvements become necessary to accommodate the original apartment. These will raise the
value of vacant lots; that, in turn, often leads to rezones. The argument that more valuable property justifies more intensive use may
be used as a rationale for approving rezones on remaining land.
(An example of the domino effect was seen when one trucker operation begot another in Riverton.)
Imagine, now, a lone citizen gazing out at an open wooded
area. Suddenly there's change: A new subdivision generates new
sewer and street assessment bills for nearby landowners, who must
share the costs; or a rezone drives a nearby farmer out of business
because he can't afford higher taxes; or the cityfolk who move in
next door drive the farmer out when they legally object to farmyard
smells and sounds. Stepping back, the observer will see subdivisions spawning shopping centers and highways, paving over rich
farmland. Take a broad view of the impact: Consider one East
Coast state that was self-sufficient in food production 30 years ago
and now ships in 80 percent of its food. Some say this phenomenon

---

*County Building and Land Development Division 1979 findings
on denial of building permit application IC-8751.

drives up food prices because food must be shipped in, incurring transportation fees.

Neither open areas nor settled communities are immune from tax impact. Rezones sow the seeds of higher property taxes. Development of raw land drives up assessed value fivefold or sixfold, according to appraiser Jack Lietz' rule of thumb. When the site goes from $1,000 to $6,000, or from $10,000 to $60,000, the assessor generally increases assessments on adjoining property. If that rezone is in a residential or open area, it may invite neighboring landowners to rezone and sell at a profit. But no rule of thumb, including Lietz', is absolute. Quality, size, shape, and use of the new building (or buildings) create various impacts. For instance, a new high-rise that blocks the view may depress assessed value and sales price of an adjoining property. A noisy nightspot may depress values, making it hard for a homeowner to sell. "Fortunately, we have a club in our neighborhood because some owners were going to put in a cocktail lounge," Spellman said.

PREHEARING HOMEWORK

Whether homeowners are worried about views or nightspots, they can band together before a hearing to protect their property values. One community group achieved a serious goal, even though the means sound Charlie Chaplinesque. Sly developers had measured the building height from the top of the slope—giving dimensions to the underneath part of the roof. One neighbor plotted with a couple of other businessmen and engineers who lived nearby. They didn't want to take a beating on their selling prices, so they countered with the helium balloon trick. Early one morning, they stealthily crept out to the site, glancing over their shoulders. Nobody hollered, "No trespassing." The first man launched the balloon to the actual height. His sidekicks on the hillside observed the impact on their property, and photographed the evidence. Waving a white handkerchief, they signaled, "Mission accomplished." They achieved knowledge of the precise impact. Thus they could speak with authority at a hearing, submit the photo, and avoid being caught by surprise when the building was constructed. Building height problems dominate land-use complaints.

Collectively, citizens can negotiate with developers. When developers come to community councils, individual irritations tend to be washed out and more-sensitive land use results, according to Dave Baugh, former county planner. Community groups can be creative and can negotiate what they want, he said, adding that community groups often get certain amenities when they ask for them.

Unfortunately, others reported, personality conflicts disable community councils at times.

Perhaps the most important prehearing homework that community groups can do is to marshal forces for the hearing. Politicians find it hard to turn a deaf ear to a jammed hearing room or to a petition bearing 1,000 names. Port of Seattle Commissioner Jack Block, speaking at a community rally against airport development, advised that the more noise you make, the more response you'll get. This rallying cry—to the loudest go the spoils—of Duwamish Peninsula Community Commission adviser Tom Gaudette was the genesis of a move for community council revitalization.

MOVES TO STRENGTHEN COMMUNITY GROUPS

The Duwamish Peninsula Community Commission is among several interests that are working to strengthen community councils. The commission, a nongovernmental citizen-advocate group, held a conference in 1979 to revitalize community councils. More-advanced communities have already gained advisory power over "area zoning" (in which the county rezones areas to bring them into closer compliance with community plans). Another move occurred when the 1978 Shoreline Community Plan Committee suggested that the county send rezone notification to officially registered community councils when an individual rezone is at hand. Then members could make recommendations to the county on whether the rezone adhered to the community plan. Shoreline's recommendation and a legislative plan echoed each other. In 1979, legislators renewed action on giving community councils legal status, as advisory arms of city and county councils. This legislation would have created a structure in which citizens could petition for a community corporation. The city or county council would hold a hearing, and could opt to hold an election on formation of the community corporation. A community council would also have veto power on certain reclassifications.

However, the state Association of Cities was a little upset by the fact that cities might have to listen to citizen groups, said sponsor state Senator Eleanor Lee, R-Seattle, after committee testimony indicated a power tug-of-war between government and the citizenry. The cities won. Senate Bill 2715 died in committee, said Lee, a former State Land Commission member.

There seemed to be a tug-of-war over housing displacement, an issue that dominates the modern city scene. Chicago's Heart of Uptown Coalition charged that governments were systematically displacing lower-income housing and creating incentives to build upper-income units, according to the March 1980 issue of the National Association of Neighborhoods' Displacement Reporter. The coalition marched on the federal courthouse, protesting delay in their suit to that effect against the Department of Housing and Urban Development (HUD) and the city. A federal judge ruled that a mediator would have to decide the case. Then Chicago promised to award the Uptown Community (represented by the Heart of Uptown Coalition) 100 certificates of federal Section 8 housing, helping fulfill its desire for its own redevelopment plan, and HUD pledged cooperation, according to the Reporter.

The National Association of Neighborhoods faced an uphill fight in its work against displacement. HUD, on behalf of the Carter administration, deliberately ignored an opportunity of incorporating language in new laws to control displacement, the Reporter stated. The association then tried to amend the U.S. Housing and Community Development Act, essentially attempting to make federal grants contingent upon effort against displacement.

Frustrations about displacement and land use have overflowed at more than one community meeting. "Rebel residents need a network" is how the typical plea goes. One community council leader, one of many who want to make things better, reasoned that consulting an "information bank" could save energy, plus teach skills. He wondered if an organization, like the Puget Sound Council of Governments, could maintain an information bank. His idea, however, died for lack of official interest. (Sample bylaws for community groups are given in Appendix D.)

3

DEAR PROTESTER

We hereby inaugurate a Dear Expert column for forlorn protesters. It is offered in a spirit of fun. Exaggerated? Perhaps.
But why not enjoy a chuckle or two along with your task.

DEAR EXPERT:

If it's rezoned multiple-family, will I have to let my mother-
in-law live in my spare bedroom?

        —FRANTIC

DEAR FRANTIC:

Only if your mother-in-law talks your wife into it.

DEAR EXPERT:

I'm so upset about a rezone proposal that I just have to ask
your advice. What's the best argument I can use at the hearing?

       —PUZZLED PROTESTER

DEAR PUZZLED:

By far, the best one is—<u>Children</u>. Plead that traffic generated by the development will threaten the Children's safety. Choke
back sobs, but don't hide your emotional distress. Tearful testimony from a young mother or teacher helps. Two helpless-looking
waifs should accompany the young mother or teacher. Only a
heartless monster would vote in favor of Traffic that will plow into
helpless Children, clustered at the bus stop.

DEAR EXPERT:
    What will happen if we let the elderly housing complex come in ?

                                            —LOVES GRANDMAS,
                                            BUT, NOT HERE

DEAR LOVES:
    The sidewalks will be rolled up for the 8 P.M. curfew, and Geritol will be the drink of the day at the neighborhood bar.

DEAR EXPERT:
    How can I prevent their water run-off from fouling my swimming pool ?

                                            —BATTLING IN BALTIMORE

DEAR BATTLING:
    You can't.

DEAR EXPERT:
    Should we show up as a group ?

                                            —NAIVE IN NEWARK, N.J.

DEAR NAIVE:
    Absolutely. Never underestimate group psychology. Always make clear you're Voters.

DEAR EXPERT:
    Do we need a fancy-talking lawyer ?

                                            —DESPERATE
                                            DUVALL, WASH.

DEAR DESPERATE:
    Not if you lose gracefully.

    You may want to add humor like this to your citizen campaign, since it is necessary to spark citizen interest. "Mix in a little fun so spirits won't sag," one savvy organizer suggested. "One of your biggest handicaps is the citizenry—apathetic, unenthusiastic, and 'much too busy to bother.'"
    Now, let's look at some serious strategy. Protesters attack the developer's application on two grounds. If they find defects in substantive issues, the tide may turn in their favor. Inconsistency with the land plan is a substantive issue. If they find a defect on procedural grounds, they may gain a psychological advantage; or they may delay the application or win the case.

A closer look at this point identifies some procedural defects. Improper notification is a procedural defect. Skilled protesters investigate whether the zoning hearing sign was posted correctly, whether notification missed property owners who should have been notified, and whether the newspaper legal notice complied with the law, in both timing and content. Further, they find out if the owner applied in another person's name, violating the owner-only requirement in their jurisdiction. (Not all jurisdictions have an owner-only requirement, however.) Finally, they see if all the requirements for the environmental check list and EIS were satisfied.

Substantive defects are more complex than procedural defects. But they boil down to fundamentals like the following:

Will the development have adverse impacts on the environment, utilities, schools, roads, or stability of the neighborhood? Will water supply or pressure be inadequate?
Is the project faithful to the density, setback, height, landscaping, and other requirements of the proposed classification?
Can the site be utilized under existing zoning?
Is the project in compliance with the land-use plan, in both map and narrative form? Does it comply with the community land-use plan?

Protesters, therefore, must ask themselves those questions.

If, however, you can't criticize inconsistency with either land-use plan, look for inconsistencies with plans of the regional government or transportation, sewer, or water district. If the project is in harmony with plans, try another angle. When the plan is ten years old, for example, argue that it's outdated because land uses have changed since its inception and new zonings have been born. Another possibility is to challenge the credibility of the plan by pointing out amendments and zoning decisions that have since been made, permitting usage contrary to the plan. Drive points home by submitting lists and graphics, complete with documentation of existing and approved zoning, dates, and location. If all else fails, seek to amend the community plan to another use, effectively denying the use at hand. One further alternative is to argue that public facilities need to catch up to development before more development can be approved. Is there any language in the plan narrative that addresses availability of public facilities? Some plans insist that public facilities be available before development is done.

MAKING FRIENDS TOE THE MARK

Let sewer and other districts know of your opposition. Attempt to get dated letters stating that the project will overburden fire, police, water, or other services. Don't hesitate to tell districts about the accumulative effect of several nearby proposals, listing the total number of units to besiege your area.

Don't be a Silent Sam or Sarah; be a watchdog. Watchdogs motivate officials to toe the mark. In the same spirit, send a letter to planners and officials, asking them to let you attend whenever they meet with the opposition. (In Washington State, the Appearance of Fairness Doctrine bans prehearing dialogue between participants and council or commission members, but a letter won't hurt.) One way to voice opposition in the planning department is to say, "I don't think this project is in compliance with the land plan." Protesters may thus evoke planning reports that are done with more depth and care than they would be if no opposition emerged. Otherwise, under the press of business, planners may incorporate developer data into the report, instead of devoting independent thinking to the report.

At the same time, build rapport in face-to-face visits. A planner whose views coincide with yours is a valuable ally. "A paid staff planner could be an unimaginative hack. Or he could be full of vigor and ideas; if this is the case, you have an extremely important ally," states the Community Action for Environmental Quality booklet, published by the Washington State Planning and Community Affairs Agency. If you follow the advice of this publication, you'll invite that planner to a community meeting:

> Ask him to give a talk to your membership on the
> problems in the area. He may have to be a bit cau-
> tious on some matters in a public presentation. For
> that reason, be sure he has an opportunity to talk
> informally with your top people.

Why is this informal get-together essential? Vital public information may never surface in the public arena, or it may be "lost" in the bigness of bureaucracy. In one case, a planner met informally, telling leaders that the site was almost zoned for elderly housing a few years ago. He detailed the history of the site, and this helped residents in their current struggle.

This same planner told residents that a HUD office had a file on the elderly housing application. Files can be gold mines. Inspect the county or city file on the project, making Xeroxes or taking notes where necessary. If staffers say that files are closed, inquire about your legal rights with the county prosecutor or city attorney.

HIDE AND SEEK

Unbeknownst to some, a developer can play hide and seek; that is, a single file may hold only part of the developer's game plan. In one case, a developer applied for a multi-unit building permit in the Department of Community Development. At the same time, he applied for residential permits in the Building and Land Development Division (BALD). Both were for the same site. A short time later, he applied for a commercial permit for an adjacent site. (His strategy was to use commercial permit approval as an argument for multi-unit zoning in his adjacent site.)

Nobody knew about applications in the other departments. Each department sent a routine inquiry to the fire district, asking whether the district was capable of serving the site. If the fire district officials hadn't known of the protest, they would have routinely processed the inquiry. Protesters, however, had done their homework. Early on they let the district know of their opposition. They were persistent, but polite. A friendly district official tipped them off when letters about the three applications came in. Not all developers play hide and seek, but the lesson is clear: a vigilant protester is less likely to get the short end of the stick.

In the EIS process, you can get short-changed even if that is not the developer's intention. It all starts out with the draft EIS that the developer submits to the county or city. County and city staff members have detected an inherent prodeveloper bias in these drafts. The bias originates with the consultant who draws up the draft, and from the consultant's desire to please the developer. That bias may be incorporated into the draft drawn up by the city or county, for it relies on the developer's material. (For more on the EIS, see Appendix E.)

You can counter the bias by submitting data on traffic impact, existing water run-off problems, or other concerns. For example, if the neighbors experience sewer, water, or drainage problems, ask them and the delivery agency to submit letters to that effect. Further, find out whether the developer neglected to point out problems on the environmental check list.

LEVERAGE

Savvy protesters press forward on other fronts, too. For one thing, they check the zoning categories to see if any offer an advantage over what the developer seeks. "Does the community, for example, have a cluster zoning ordinance?" asks the Community Action for Environmental Quality. (Planned-unit developments

[PUD] represent one form of cluster development. PUDs provide incentive by giving higher density, in exchange for more open space.) "Cluster development is not only good for the community; it happens to be good for the developer too. . . . If you're going to support cluster zoning, developers should not pressure against other conservation measures, as by reflex, many are apt to do. . . ."

In short, look for leverage. You can't work out differences unless you know what the developer needs. If you can supply that, you can exert leverage. "In many communities, the developer is thought of as the principal enemy. He needs friends," the booklet states. First, "it is in his self interest to go a good part of the way to meet your wishes. . . ." Second, "since he needs your support, you are in an excellent bargaining position. Make the most of it. At the very least you should get a truce from the developer."

You should also make the most of public meetings. Few do. According to the booklet:

> The most common error is to hold the meeting in too large a hall. It is extraordinary how many times local groups will squander the potential effect by poor mechanics.

> It's relative size that counts. Four hundred people turn up—a fine turnout. But it doesn't look it at all. The audience dribbles away.

> But put the same program in a hall that can just barely hold them and you have an entirely different equation. The place is packed. You even have some standees. There is excitement in the air.

> Speakers rise to such an occasion. So will the audience. So will the press. The press is a tool to be cultivated.

> The best way to get good newspaper, radio and TV coverage is to make news yourself.

> Don't scorn gimmicks; if they genuinely dramatize the issue, they are extremely useful. The Smokey Bear campaign is an example; another is the walk along the Chesapeake and Ohio Canal led by Justice William Douglas.

Of course, you aren't trying to prevent forest fires, but you can modify borrowed techniques to suit your needs.

One thing that is common to all citizen campaigns is that bad breaks occur. Don't give up. Instead, capitalize on bad breaks. See if they sharpen your cause, rally your cohort. A bad break may give you a more tangible cause around which to unify your support. According to Community Action for Environmental Quality, some of the country's outstanding citizen programs owe a large part of their momentum to the necessity of a crash program to fight off highway engineers or other opponents.

In summary, your task is to rally residents so hearings will reflect their enthusiasm and their numbers. Coach residents to stand up in a bloc at the hearing so officials will instantly be informed that a large number of votes ride on their decision.

THE HEARING

It's a two-way ride. Hearing officials won't vote for your side if you insult them. Community Action for Environmental Quality counsels that, "there is no surer way to court failure than to start off with truculence. . . . Convince politicians that there is strong citizen support for your cause and they will want to be for it. Politicians like to look good. Help them."

One way to help them is to speak in terms of the public good: Never say, "The building will block my view"; instead say, "The height of the building is incompatible with the character of the neighborhood." Similarly, never say, "Those no-good profiteers will make us taxpayers pay for the public services for their development"; instead say, "Inadequate public facilities to serve the development mean significant public expenditures that will not be returned through anticipated tax revenue."

Espousing the public good is like wearing white collars and tweed suits. Being devilish is like wearing short skirts. Documented, it can attract attention. Devilish citizens who hope to discredit developers submit government records of their code violations and photos of their run-down, poorly constructed developments elsewhere—or point out that the developers never responded to written invitations to get together with citizens and discuss the project.

In a more positive vein, you may want to submit photos depicting your tidy homes and stable community. Strike a positive stance by submitting data indicating a disproportionate share of multi-units in your neighborhood. Ask that multi-units be more evenly distributed among neighborhoods. Never say, "We're against development."

The best way to let officials know that your neighborhood has been deluged with development is with graphic art. Colored tape can outline the residential community; flashy-colored tape can mark developments that have intruded within the past five years.

Print "56 units" or the appropriate figure next to each development.
It doesn't hurt to use a different color to denote rejected develop-
ments, with the name and reason for rejection printed next to each.
Other good arguments include:

1. Data on high traffic impact
2. Information on how the lack of sidewalks and school-crossing
   guards and heavy reliance on street parking impair the safety
   of children
3. Letters from the education association or principal on teacher-
   student ratio, and estimated impact from the development
4. Photos of water run-off damage already inflicted on the neighborhood, accompanied by the argument that more asphalt (and
   less vegetation) would only accelerate the problem
5. Campaign disclosure records showing sizeable contributions
   from the developer to the councilman on the hearing panel

Further, much of the information in Chapter 7 is applicable
to this chapter. Conversely, developers can benefit by reading the
material in this chapter.

THE LONG-RANGE VIEW

Scrutiny doesn't end for savvy protesters once the developer
gets a nod of approval from government—or once the developer is
turned down. On the nuts-and-bolts level: "Legal authority may
have prevented a construction company from dumping excess dirt
into an adjoining lake and our yards. The supervisor would never
order that done. But he intentionally didn't order the bulldozer
operator to not order dumping in the lake and our yards. So the
operator dumped dirt and brush. No one had knowingly committed
a misdeed," one resident recalled. Watchful citizens kept an eye
on this actual incident, tipping off the building inspector. Correc-
tive action was taken.
Scrutiny won't pay dividends, though, unless residents are
organized. "The vital task is to build on the momentum [of ad hoc
neighborhood meetings]. Harness those energies for a long-pull
job—the kind that will make ad hoc groups and emergency meetings
less necessary," advises Community Action for Environmental
Quality.
To harness energies, appoint a watchdog group (or groups)
for budget and land-plan hearings; for vigilance on open space; and
for opportunity to be heard before highway, sewer, and other plans
harden. (Conversely, developers who want to have a voice in what

happens should join local affiliates of master builders or construction councils.)

Another long-term move is to investigate and utilize grants. HUD paid two-thirds of the cost of various community planning studies, for example.* Of course, not everyone feels comfortable about using government money.

Still another long-term strategy is to convince government to encourage citizen participation. Here's a smorgasbord of techniques to choose from:

The District of Columbia has operated a registry process, through which advisory neighborhood groups received notice of current issues. This process, like the following, may change from time to time.

Fairfax County, Virginia, published weekly agendas of certain meetings.

Salem, Oregon, officially recognized neighborhood groups if they met certain criteria.

Friendship Heights, Massachusetts, had the planning commission adopt a plan reportedly developed by citizens.

San Jose, California, citizens voted through the telephone system— instant voting in an age of instant products.

Each technique, in some way, aims for accountability. To insist on accountability, citizens might want to borrow a technique used in Coventry, England. Here, the planning department was directed to respond specifically to input, stating the rationale for changing or not changing the land plan.

Universally, the basic question is: How can the community control its destiny while the government affords property owners the maximum use of their private-property rights? Inherently, that question involves compromise. As Saul D. Alinsky observes in his Rules for Radicals:

---

*While grant criteria and availability vary through the years, these sources are some of those that citizens utilize: HUD's Open Space Program for acquisition; HUD's beautification grants; HUD's sewer and water grants; the Land Water Conservation Fund Act of 1965 for acquisition; federal Economic Development Administration grants for depressed areas; the U.S. Army Corps of Engineers' Beach Erosion Control Program; the U.S. Department of Agriculture and Farmers Home Administration aid to rural areas; the U.S. Bureau of Sports Fisheries (Pittman-Robertson and Dingell-Johnson programs) for acquisition; state or local open-space programs.

Compromise is another word that carries shades of
weakness, vacillation, betrayal of ideals, surrender
of moral principles. In the old culture, where vir-
ginity was a virtue, one referred to a woman's being
"compromised." The word is generally regarded as
ethically unsavory and ugly. But to the organizer,
compromise is a key and beautiful word.

"COME, NOW, LET US REASON
TOGETHER"—ISAIAH 1:18

"Negotiated settlements are the wave of the future in land
use," lawyer Judith Runstad told a crowd of 1,000 at a land-use
seminar. What this means is that a developer and a citizen group
negotiate a written pact that records trade-offs. One citizen group
won lower density by swapping a pledge of no protest. The developer won government approval for construction, escaping costly
delays. "Negotiated settlements are good deals for developers
because they can say to decision makers, 'Both sides agree, except for one small point—regarding left-turn lanes,'" said Joel
Haggard, a lawyer who represents developers.

Basically, the question boils down to, Why battle when you
can bargain? Opponents pulled their chairs up to the bargaining
table in the following cases, which illustrate the wide range of disputes that may be resolved through negotiation. The first case
involves Washington State. "We require the Washington Public
Power Supply System (WPPSS) to bargain in good faith with a community when there will be a social-economic impact from siting a
power plant," said Bill Fitch of the Washington State Energy Facility Site Evaluation Council. To date, WPPSS has paid $15 million
in impact payments. "The law calls for compensation for loss of
wild or aquatic life," Fitch explained. "Fish, for example, were
given as compensation for Columbia River fish loss. If parties do
not bargain in good faith, they must come before our council. Then
we have to prod them."

In Nebraska, the National Wildlife Federation and utility companies were at odds over the Platte River dam plan. The federation feared damage to a crucial stopover point on the migration
path of the whooping crane. Ultimately, the utilities established a
$7.5 million trust fund to buy land and water rights and to pay for
research, on behalf of the birds, according to Patrick Parenteau,
a director of the federation.

Washington State utilized the same principle. Here, Dixy Lee
Ray, then governor, recommended compensating monies for the

city of Monroe to help offset costs from a proposed 500-bed prison. Prisons strain local law enforcement, prosecutor budgets, sewers, and services.

Beyond Monroe, sewers are sore spots with communities. When septic-tank pollution threatened scenic Payette Lake in Idaho, it was clear that sewers were needed. Fortunately, federal aid was forthcoming, provided a land-use plan was drawn up. Affected residents, however, felt disfranchised when the city adopted a land-use plan within three days—without hearings, according to Gerald Cormick, University of Washington (UW) Institute of Environmental Mediation director. Unhappy homeowners went to court. Mediation ended the stalemate, fortunately. Cormick explained that the city of McCall agreed to establish a zoning and planning commission composed of Payette Lake homeowners for the affected area.

Mediation is distinguished from direct negotiations because it involves an impartial third party. A mediator does not decide a case but, instead, listens to opposing camps, assisting them in reconciling their own differences. "[Mediation] can legitimize conflict and provide an arena within which shifting social priorities and power centers have an opportunity to interact," Cormick told the National Association of Environmental Professionals at a Washington, D.C., conference. He said the Environmental Mediation Project in Madison, Wisconsin, also works on cases like Payette Lake.

Smaller-scale disputes may also be resolved. For example, the Continental Plaza Association of Seattle wanted to bulldoze low-income housing to build luxury condominiums. Eventually, pressure produced a pact. Continental Plaza Association agreed to restore two old buildings nearby to provide low-rent housing for displaced renters, according to Neisco "Al" Moscatel of the firm.

International Land Corp., Ltd., also bucked the housing displacement issue. Then the Canadian firm agreed to rent 4 units in its 61-unit luxury condo in Seattle to displaced tenants for $90 per month, plus cost-of-living increases tied to the consumer price index (CPI). In addition, International Land agreed to build 6 apartment units nearby, renting them for $150 per month, plus CPI adjustments. Developers paid $350 in relocation costs to each tenant evicted from the old Kelleher House, also on the condo site. For work on negotiations, the firm compensated the First Hill Community Council $2,500, and, in return, the council did not block the building permit application for the 17-story condo. Settlements such as this one permit both sides to score points, rather than gamble with defeat before the city or county council.

Courts are an impetus to bargaining, too. In court, one side wins, one side loses. Clogged calendars mean delays, which cost developers money. At the bargaining table, issues may be resolved sooner. Legal fees shrink.

Ethical questions are more complex. So is gamesmanship. "Putting this item in a pact is great for the developer because people will feel like they are getting something," lawyer Peter Buck said, referring to an item homeowners could get—even without a pact. "Peter, you did not have to say that!" admonished another developer lawyer, reluctant to disclose tricks of the trade.

Cutting to the heart of the ethical question, some citizens won't negotiate because they believe the environment cannot be traded off; others say they won't accept a "bribe" to permit environmental damage. "It has sort of a 'murder for hire' aura," commented Jeffrey Roughgarden, then a Stanford University economist-engineer research associate; but "in-kind" compensation diminishes the aura, he added.

In-kind compensation was the trade-off when the Port of Everett agreed to preserve one acre of land on Jetty Island for each acre consumed by development; or when the Port of Grays Harbor agreed to swap 2,500 acres of wetland to the state Department of Game, in exchange for being allowed to develop 500 other acres. "It's more complex than 2,500 for 500 acres," declared Washington Environmental Council's Liz Greenhagen. "We've found new evidence that the 500 acres is a habitat. We also feel there is political pressure to get the case implemented."

Negotiations can bog down in political quicksand—or from citizen nitpicking, mistrust, or misgivings. David Brower, then Sierra Club executive director, said he resigned on May 3, 1969, then founded Friends of the Earth, after differences over siting a nuclear power plant in Diablo Canyon, California. Even the Sierra Club board had misgivings about a siting agreement with Pacific Gas & Electric Company, issuing a statement that it had "made a mistake of principle and policy in attempting to bargain away an area of unique scenic beauty," according to Brower.

Negotiations can also bog down because of the way the laws are written. "A new federal-state project is under way involving a couple of states," said Cormick, the UW mediator. "Our project aims to redraft some state and federal legislation to encourage settlements, and to discourage lawsuits." Settlements, not stalemates, appear to be the emerging trend.

CHECK LISTS

Participants should examine the following check lists to see if a potential pact will safeguard their interests. Aramburu supplied the homeowners' list; Runstad modified the developers' check list, a composite from lawyers.

"To prevent pitfalls," Aramburu cautioned, "parties should work with an experienced lawyer when negotiating. Enter warily, only after becoming familiar with all the issues and personalities."

Settlement Agreement: Citizens' Provisions

1. Bind future parties:
   a. Bind all future owners by making the agreement run with the land.
   b. Make sure the agreement is shown on the title report.
   c. Spell out how future owners of the property will be bound by the agreement.

     d. Require the present owner to provide the agreement to the future owner.

2. Avoid vague terms:
     a. Provide specific provisions for what will be done. Attach plans or diagrams, if necessary.
     b. Set a time limit for performance. If amenities are to be provided, insist that amenities will be installed before use or occupation of site.
     c. Spell out standards of performance for any continuing obligations. For example, "Vegetation [use generic name] will be maintained and kept in healthy condition."

3. Insure monitoring:
     a. Specify how reports will be made to citizens on progress of performance.
     b. State that a disinterested professional will monitor an obligation. For example, a competent engineer will check water-pollution levels.
     c. Say that the developer will pay for monitoring.

4. Set enforcement guidelines:
     a. Find that local government, impacted citizens, or outside parties have enforcement power.
     b. State that, in the case of a court battle, fess for legal counsel and expert witnesses will be awarded to the successful party. Add that this clause will be separately enforceable if the developer complies at the eleventh hour before a trial.
     c. Provide a court injunction to enforce the agreement if the developer does not comply with the agreement, an injunction which either prohibits the developer from using the property or specifically requires the developer to do the things she or he is supposed to do.
     d. Spell out: "All provisions are material and substantial and may be enforced by injunction."
     e. State agreement of both parties to acceptance of service for any summons and for participation in a court hearing within a short period of time from a summons.
     f. Agree to enter binding arbitration, with preservation of original "status quo," when noncompliance by either party can't be resolved through discussion.

Settlement Agreement: Developers' Provisions

1. Identify the position and authority of the parties on both sides.
2. Recite the background of the dispute and the issue(s).

3. Attach the approved plan as an exhibit to the agreement. This plan need only be a schematic, with the developer's right to modify, subject to certain constraints.

4. List all permits, followed by a clause saying that the list is noninclusive.

5. State the opposing group's support for the project, as well as a group pledge not to interfere or cause interference. "The group," in some cases, will be individuals.

6. Set a time limit on the agreement, with the developer's right to extend the agreement as long as he or she makes good-faith application for permits. List a time schedule for permit processing, with this good-faith provision.

7. Cite a designated authorized group for approval of major revisions, and state a time period for approvals.

8. Forbid appeals on State Environmental Policy Act (SEPA) or National Environmental Policy Act (NEPA) grounds.

9. Define the project—and agreed-upon reasonable alternatives to be discussed—if an EIS is slated.

10. Obtain governmental recognition of the settlement agreement.

4

PLANNING, PLOTTING,
AND PUBLIC RELATIONS

Learning the nuts and bolts of the zoning game is like reading a primer on "the three Ps"—planning, plotting, and public relations. If land-use players used the three Ps, they'd stand a better chance of winning. If they plotted, they'd use information and agencies to their advantage. Instead, they often ignore staff and data. (Staff means county employees, ranging from planners to traffic engineers.) If they planned, they'd embark on hearing preparation early, learning a lesson from the experts who lay the groundwork for success. If they used public relations, they'd give concise hearing testimony. Instead, several speakers usually parade to the stand, lapsing into repetitious testimony. Emotional outbursts are commonplace. Yet hearing officials favored those who relied on evidence, not emotion, in the following case histories. This chapter opens with tips from zoning experts, then moves into case histories that illustrate the nuts and bolts. The chapter closes with ways to defuse the dynamite—reduce the tension between developers and residents.

PREHEARING HOMEWORK

People are their own worst enemy, lawyer Jerry Hillis finds. They constantly think there are pay-offs, favoritism, secret meetings, and a conspiracy against them, he said, adding that that is just not the case. People ignore staff members and fail to get the facts, he finds.

"Yet, a little grandma, in some respects, can be more effective than the experienced downtown attorney—if that grandma is willing to approach the problem objectively, find out the facts, go to the staff, and ask them for information," advised this downtown attorney. One grandma, Margaret Brittenham, regrets that she didn't even know enough to go to the staff and ask for the prehearing report on the proposed rezone for a 22-unit apartment building. This staff report favored the rezone; her band of neighbors went down to defeat.

If you lend an ear to what Hillis says, you'll follow this sequence: receive rezone or reclassification notice; query staff on when the prehearing report will be released; query staff on whether there will be a hearing; query staff on whether zoning and number of units per acre adhere to county land plans and whether traffic and drainage pose any problem. When the prehearing report runs against them, the experts immediately work up arguments and evidence to undermine the findings at the hearing. In short, they do their homework. The experts go one step farther. They try to work out differences with the opposition before the hearing, knowing that the most convincing evidence is testimony that many or all differences have been resolved.

Use the new style of negotiating, instead of the old style of "out-talking them" at the hearing, urged developer Doug Webb of Subdivision Management Inc. Webb told a conference of builders why negotiation is essential to prevent a showdown in the hearing or court arena. It is easier to get acquainted with those folks in the design stage, he explained. Sit down with them; ask them what they'd like to see, Webb advised. In effect, see how the shoe fits the other foot. You are going to meet with them at some time—in court, in a hearing, or in a living room, he went on. The living room is better; things are less tense. Otherwise, by the time they reach the hearing, "they've got their guns oiled," he warned. By the time the hearing arrives, the position of the county, developer, and residents has hardened.

Hillis has instilled the spirit of negotiating into his whole law firm. The first clue to his approach came during a conversation with a lawyer from Hillis' firm. The purpose of the call was to get his client's side of a case destined to be a landmark in the county. "Yes," the law partner confirmed, "I did call two members of the Highline Community Council, but I couldn't convince them to understand our side." He added that the firm's policy is to explore issues with the opposition before a hearing. Continuing to discuss his side, the lawyer mentioned that he might ask Hillis to handle the coming hearing on the complex case. Hillis did—and won.

Jerry Hillis. County courthouse sources kept referring to his name. "He's not abrasive, like ——, another brilliant lawyer," said one. "And when a close case comes down to the wire, he's got what it takes to win." Hillis plants the seeds of success in the pre-hearing stage. Negotiation is helpful in certain cases, he finds. Negotiation entails the spirit of compromise. There has been a compromise in almost every controversial case that has gone through, Hillis said, referring to his developer clients.

A typical dialogue begins when he calls a homeowner. Hillis said, "John Doe owns the land near you, and he is proposing an apartment house. He wants to know your concerns at this stage, and hopefully, work them out." Dialogue proves fruitful. In one case, he said, he met with neighbors about 20 times over six months, talking about sidewalks, landscaping, and the location of the parking lot and building. Plans were revised from 92 to 78 units, then a formal agreement between both camps was drawn up, according to Hillis. Clear sailing lay ahead. Owners of the $60,000 homes nearby were receptive. Dialogue, however, is not always effective. Hillis has observed recent stiffening of residents' attitudes, and former Yakima Planning Director Fred Stouder observed that residents are demanding more and more. He pleaded for less selfishness from all land-use players.

Dialogue didn't work in one rezone case. Sometime after the zoning examiner hearing, the developer's representative met with angry opponents and tried to defuse emotion by explaining the builder's position in favor of apartments. He failed. Angry residents, on two occasions, formed a caravan and drove to the builder's home, located in an expensive waterfront neighborhood. They knocked at his door. He wasn't at home. Undaunted, they passed out flyers to his neighbors, stating, "Would you want this apartment built next door? He won't talk to us." His home phone was printed on the flyer, along with a warning they would return. They continued to agitate by bringing a stuffed dummy to the council hearing. Later, Hillis reflected on the case, for he represented the builder at the council hearing. Someone told them to bring that dummy, someone told them to march on the council, Hillis charged. The residents were as insulting to officials and to the process as any he had seen, Hillis declared. Then the insult backfired; the council ruled against them. Furthermore, it was clear that polarization had occurred. Hillis said he had ceased negotiation efforts.

EXIT: THE WRONG WAY;
ENTER: THE RIGHT WAY

Insults backfire; authorities become alienated. Hillis avoids even small "insults." For he knows that zealous, antagonistic behavior rubs government officialdom the wrong way, just as it does

anyone else. But many forget that decision makers, too, are human
beings who respond well to considerate behavior. Yet, he said,
people voice these insults: "You are not listening. . . . You do not
understand. . . . You are more interested in such and such, than
such and such." He avoids even such small personal "insults."
Hillis inspires confidence, he acknowledged, by being reasonable
and openly up-front with land-use players and with officeholders.

People become their own worst enemies when they fail to present their case effectively at the hearing. The biggest problem
people have is not organizing themselves carefully to make a concise presentation, land-use lawyer Richard Aramburu warned.
People just don't appreciate that a hearing can be a desperately bor-
ing task for officials who would rather be home watching television,
he said. Put yourself in their shoes, he advised. Richard Babcock,
author of The Zoning Game, puts it this way, "Judges find zoning a
monumental bore, most lawyers consider it a nuisance, and planners
treat it as a cretinous member of the planning family, about whom
the less said, the better."

DECISIONS MADE ON A POLITICAL BASIS

Above all, land-use players should bear in mind how land use
is defined. Zoning is not a black-and-white matter with cut-and-
dried decisions. Decisions are discretionary. Land use is an issue
of negotiation and politics, Stouder said. Aramburu agreed. Land-
use decisions are basically political, Aramburu stressed. A lot of
decisions are still being made on an almost purely political basis—
without necessarily dealing with the facts, he said, adding that he
would like to eliminate the politics. But county Building and Land
Development Division (BALD) Director Ed Sand disagreed. In many
parts of the country, zoning is abused and is used politically, he admitted, adding that that is not true in King County.

However, some call the Environmental Impact Statement (EIS)
process a political push and shove. The EIS document tells what impact a development will have on traffic counts, water run-off, and
more. Citizen critics complain that developers inject bias when
their consultants compile the document (subject to final review by
the government). On the other hand, developers complain that residents misuse the EIS by injecting undue delay into the process. (For
more on the EIS, see Appendix E.)

Without doubt, the EIS process is shaped by the invisible hand
of the court. Here's how Charles Linstad, county environmental
specialist, analyzes the invisible influence: Sizeable projects generally demand an EIS. The county is reluctant to deny a building

permit on the basis of EIS information, unless environmental damage can't be diminished to an acceptable level. The county must have clear-cut reasons to deny a permit. If those reasons are hazy, the developer challenges the county in court—and wins. Typically, when the county denies a permit, the developer "hits" the county with a legal document called a writ of certiorari, Linstad said. That's followed up by a writ of mandamus, which says the government must give the developer a permit, he explained. He observed that rulings that refute the county's findings prove embarrassing. Clearly, the court challenges the protester to dig up evidence of damaging impacts. It's up to the protesters to build a case that will obviate court action, because government is too busy.

HIDDEN HARBOR

Hidden Harbor protesters tackled the challenge of building a strong case, successfully working against construction of Hidden Harbor Hotel. When realtor Vince Varacalli requested a building permit for a 78-unit hotel on March 17, 1978, he ignited a protest that embroiled the community for two years. Here are the highlights of the step-by-step work that unfolded during those two years.* Residents:

1. Seized the opportunity of getting an EIS by petitioning
2. Searched for procedural defects in the permit application procedure; finding none, they searched for procedural defects in the most recent rezone on the site, then plotted to use one defect to put the county on the defensive (see reference to the 1968 rezone later in this section)
3. Checked whether zoning was inconsistent with county land plans
4. Researched other substantive issues—water run-off, water supply, traffic
5. Plotted against water district expansion to ensure that water would be inadequate for the site
6. Made government representatives toe the mark

---

*Note that the main difference between the rezoning process and the EIS process is that rezone hearings are automatic, while EIS hearings are optional. Otherwise, land-use players can use these case histories for guidance in rezone battles. Instead of a lengthy EIS report, rezones often have a prehearing report, essentially a mini-EIS.

The citizenry mounted a campaign that is a primer of the three Ps: plotting, planning, and public relations. The community exercised public relations by letting the county know—loud and clear—of its opposition. Upon finding a building permit application posted on-site, residents plotted, quickly collecting 300 names on a petition of opposition. Petitions were hastily dispatched to county officials. Then the county mandated an EIS, causing Varacalli to conclude that petitions triggered the EIS requirement.

"When the county observed the opposition, it forced the county into the position of asking for an EIS," he declared. "If the county hadn't, it would be liable to a court suit from protesters. When asked to state his view of the issues, Varacalli declined to comment except to say, "I don't care how many petitions were signed. No one ever phoned me voicing opposition." He plunged ahead with his work, hiring a consultant to compile a $7,000 draft EIS for a 68-unit motel. The county had scaled down his initial application for a 78-unit hotel because of insufficient parking. No rezone was necessary for the 1.9-acre site, south of Seattle, because it was already zoned for multi-units.

In August, each side embarked on its own strategy. Varacalli's August 22 letter offered to sell the county about one-third of the site, plus adjoining property he owned. His plan fizzled when Bob Jacobs of the county turned him down, saying that the site was too close to an existing park. Observers wondered whether Varacalli was trying to encourage the county to grant the permit. Meanwhile, cinnamon rolls and cynicism were served up one August morning at the home of Carol Clos, a protest leader. About ten worried residents listened to Marlene Herold of the Duwamish Peninsula Community Commission, a nongovernmental citizen-advocate group. Residents heard Herold say that developers must be cut off at the pass. She often draws on her miniature cigar, just as she draws a long bead on developers.

"It's like guerrilla warfare; you have to sit down and 'strategize,'" she advised. She also drew a bead on bureaucrats, saying that they have reneged on what they told individuals at times. However, she added, there's a strategy to cut developers off at the pass and to prevent reneging. Call a community meeting, inviting officials who are above the pass-the-buck position, Herold urged; make bureaucrats respond to a group. Put them under the gun—ask them how their department will respond to the EIS, she suggested. The EIS is circulated to various agencies for their comments on any adverse impacts.

"Force a traffic engineer to disclose what traffic conditions are. If he can't say they are O.K., he can't write O.K. on the EIS," Herold said. "It sounds like traffic is your biggie." Ask the de-

partment of public works for traffic counts and projections and ask
the nearby Highline Community College for enrollment forecasts
and related traffic projections, Herold advised. She suggested on-
listing allies, like the college president. Residents subsequently
had a nearby city rally to their cause. Research and allies were
necessary to build a strong case, Herold said, since residents faced
an uphill fight.

In an aside, Herold reflected a bit, saying, "You sure have a
beautiful view in this area. You can bet the developer is eyeing it.
When you run into the county council, courts, and politicians, they'll
say that you shouldn't be so selfish." She doesn't see resistance as
selfish; she sees developers as greedy. "One of the reasons that
I'm here with you today is that I hate developers," Herold confided.
    Residents were keenly aware that they faced an uphill fight,
having lost an autumn bid to annex the community to the neighboring
city of Normandy Park. The Hidden Harbor application had ignited
the annexation drive, but Normandy Park refused annexation because
it didn't want apartments either.

Despite discouragement, protesters pressed forward. They searched unsuccessfully for procedural defects in notification. Then they spent hours at the courthouse building department, reading the files on the site. Finally, they found what appeared to be a procedural defect: no apparent notification of the 1968 rezone from single-family to multi-unit zoning. Their conclusion was based on county records (indicating that no residents attended rezone hearings) and on later conversations with old-timers adjacent to the site. To put the county on the defensive, they went to the newspapers, armed with old rezone reports. They gained excellent press coverage and achieved restoration of single-family zoning two years later (see discussion below). Their outcry put officialdom on notice—in effect, making "friends toe the mark." Inviting government representatives to community meetings served the same purpose. Next, residents researched land plans (available at libraries and the building department). When they discovered zoning was inconsistent with the community plan, they never let government representatives forget that. Throughout, residents kept an eye on the site, checking out traffic and drainage patterns.

In October, they saw construction begin. Stunned, residents pelted county officials with calls, fearing that motel construction had begun before a decision was made on a building permit. The county building permit inspector supervisor assured the complainants that the construction was legal: Varacalli was ringing the Hidden Harbor site with duplexes. Even though adjacent land was zoned single-family, a county zoning code quirk permitted a narrow ring of duplexes around RM 900, the existing multiple-family zoning of the Hidden Harbor site.

Suspicion grew. Residents called another community meeting, raising $1,025 to retain a lawyer. The $1,025 defense fund was collected from 44 families at the meeting. One man took on the task of heading a fund-raising committee that would march door to door. Protesters at the meeting designated another member, with business connections, to search out a land-use lawyer. He came back to a subsequent meeting with a slate of three; the community favored Richard Aramburu. Even so, turning to a lawyer wasn't an easy decision. Reluctant residents fired off a barrage of questions at each other. "Do we have to hire a lawyer? When is the right time? How can we prevent excessive charges? How about approving a limited fee?" One citizen reasoned that by clamping a lid on the fee protesters impose a tactical disadvantage on themselves, since a developer who is privy to that knowledge will conclude he or she won't be taken to court. Other questions were answered to their satisfaction. Additional answers came from Aramburu, who said the time to head to a lawyer may be when one senses something is being done that is not right, or when confusion about the case can't be untangled through normal channels. Aramburu and experienced campaigners advise retaining a land-use lawyer.

Residents can get the most mileage per dollar if they do some of the legwork, like obtaining public documents from the courthouse, according to Aramburu. He said lawyers can handle some cases on an advisory basis for lower legal fees. He charges an estimated $500-$1,000 to steer citizens in the right direction. That's less than the minimum bill of about $1,000 he estimated for EIS work, or $7,000 for court cases. It is emphasized that these rough figures can vary. Legal work done by another lawyer on an EIS cost $3,000. Aramburu has heard pleas for frugality before, since they're typically expressed by citizen groups. However, he said, residents must expect to spend a significant amount when they're fighting a developer. What people don't understand is that condo developers, for example, may pay $40,000 for a lawyer to protect their $1 million investment and their $300,000 potential profit; you just can't expect to stop them with a turn of your hand, Aramburu explained.

It took more than a turn of their hands for protesters to stop Varacalli. Residents fought him on three fronts: with people power; with EIS research; and with a precise petition. When Aramburu entered the case, he drew up a legal petition and instructed residents to gather 1,000 signatures for presentation at the coming EIS hearing. They went door-to-door, finally collecting 1,000 signatures. The petition stated:

We, the undersigned, do strongly object to the construction of the Hidden Harbor Apartment/Motel at Fifth Place South and South 216th Street because the proposed development:
1) Violates the terms of the Highline Communities Plan which designates this area for single-family residences;
2) Places a high-density use in a single-family neighborhood;
3) Will create potential drainage and pollution problems;
4) Is in an area with landslide and seismic hazards;
5) Will aggravate already serious traffic problems on Des Moines Way South, Marine View Drive South, First Avenue South and South 216th Street;
6) Will introduce a transient use (motel) into a stable residential neighborhood;
7) Will cause property values to decline;

We further respectfully petition King County and
the King County Council to:
1) Hold a public hearing on the environmental impact of the proposal pursuant to WAC 197-10-
480 (2) [WACs are rules that tell agencies how
to administer laws];
2) Rezone the subject property to RS-7200 (single-
family residences).

Simultaneously, Varacalli and residents were working on the
draft EIS. Procedurally, Varacalli was to submit a draft EIS to the
county. Then residents would inspect the draft, writing counter
comments. They hoped to counter any bias. The county environmental analyst who was the final author advised them to "submit
facts, not opinion." To gather facts, several citizen teams plunged
into their work. Each team relied on residents who had a vested interest in donating their expertise in engineering, hydrology (water),
and other areas. Residents' efforts in the six months it took to
hammer out a draft included contacting the Washington Department
of Ecology. They asked department employees to monitor a salmon-
spawning stream below the hillside site because silt from water run-
off could pollute the stream. No damage was detected, however.
Residents' research paid off when the team that attended Water
District 54 meetings discovered that water supply was insufficient
for serving the site. To enlarge supply and pressure, the district
then conducted a drive (which residents resisted) for a new water
tank. The district sent letters to the community, pleading water in-
adequacies. Then protesters turned that letter in to the county as
evidence of why a permit should be denied.
Courteously, one team visited Charles Linstad, raising questions about traffic and about zoning inconsistency with the community
plan. Some of their traffic criticisms had validity, Linstad con-
ceded. "When you're heading south, you're committing suicide in
making left-hand turns. Traffic access is impossible," he said,
adding that he was optimistic that changes could be hammered out
with county and state engineers, clearing the way for the permit.
One of Varacalli's revised EIS reports contained an addendum with
traffic improvement plans. Personally, Linstad felt the permit
would be issued, subject to resolution of the traffic and run-off problems. Linstad's recommendation passed to Ed Sand, BALD director,
who made the final decision. Residents wrote to BALD, requesting
and getting an evening hearing in the community, instead of the customary daytime hearing in the courthouse.
The hearing pitted two strong, stubborn personalities against
each other. Each was unaccustomed to compromise. The career of

Varacalli, the son of an immigrant Italian shoe repairman, is a
Horatio Alger success story. He owns several hotels and parlays
investors' money from Canada, Arabia, and China into higher dividends. Jeanne Moeller had been elected president when the residents' group decided at a community meeting to incorporate. She
is equally proud of achievements. "We're visible proof that the
American dream works. One of my grandfathers was a street
sweeper, one was a blacksmith. We girls all went to college," she
said.

She and other leaders marshaled a huge, enthusiastic crowd
at the evening EIS hearing in the spring of 1979. They and their
lawyer made a concise presentation, based on research already discussed in this chapter. Entered as exhibits were the water district
letter and photographs of water run-off erosion. Also entered was
a photograph of the 12-foot by 25-foot, two-story house that Varacalli
had built on an adjacent lot during the scrap. They dubbed it "The
Spite House" in an attempt to discredit him.

After the hearing, BALD Director Ed Sand denied the permit,
primarily because of inadequate water flow for fire protection. Adverse impact from traffic was another major reason for rejecting
the permit application. Overall public costs of the project would be
greater than the revenues; the added public costs to remedy the
traffic and water problems would result in a substantial financial
impact that could not be mitigated, Sand said. Additionally, he
faulted multi-unit use, saying it was inconsistent with the community
plan.

Dissatisfied, residents continued to write to the county, asking for restoration of single-family zoning; for the ghost of the 1968
rezone from single-family to multi-unit haunted the case, from
start to finish. In the 1978 protest, citizen leaders pointed a finger
of blame at the county, saying it had failed to notify adjoining owners
of the application to "spot zone" the site in 1968. Three longtime
owners were among those who insisted that the county never notified
them of any hearing. No citizens attended the February 27, 1968,
or April 2, 1968, public hearing, according to county records. On
April 2, 1968, the planning commission rezones the property to
multi-units, despite a planning department recommendation against
this "spot zone." At the new hearing, the zoning examiner said,
"The 1968 zoning action was based on misinformation." Commissioners thought the site was adjacent to the Des Moines business district,
he said. In reality, this site was not adjacent to a commercial core,
the examiner said; thus the zoning action failed to comply with land-
use policy. His recommendation passed to the county council. On
June 2, 1980, the council took the rare step of downzoning the site
to single-family zoning. The council rarely initiates a downzone on
a single piece of property.

Looking back, perhaps the best example of what not to do is provided by the indifference in the neighborhood in the 1960s. Lack of rezone notification didn't prevent residents from regularly inquiring about whether any developer had applied for a building permit for the 1.9-acre site. It was ripe for development. If residents had scouted out the status of that empty lot years ago, they probably would have rebuffed the 1968 rezone. On the other hand, the 1978 scrap aptly demonstrates what protesters should do. They should try to get an EIS for nonroutine, complex cases. Without an EIS, community input is limited to a few letters on the building permit application. These residents correctly consulted with outside experts (Herold, Aramburu). Furthermore, they effectively used people power, from petitioning to turning out en masse for the hearing. Next, they raised questions about land plans and traffic and water impact, thus encouraging the water district, the county, and especially Linstad to toe the mark. (Linstad is a respected official who would toe the mark, regardless of prodding, but the point is made to demonstrate that protesters must raise questions with Linstad's counterpart in other areas.) During the hearing, protesters argued factually about the water and traffic situation. Finally, they proved that working long-range pays off, for the county restored single-family zoning.

HIGHLAND VILLAGE

Hidden Harbor exemplifies the plots and subplots of the zoning fame, but Highland Village shines when it comes to hearing presentations. BALD Director Ed Sand said those who argued against construction of the 646-unit Highland Village Apartment did a better job than most protesters—and they won.

George Peterson of Polygon Corporation, Canada, applied in the spring of 1978 for Highland Village building permits. No rezone was needed because the 30-acre site, near Seattle, was appropriately zoned for multi-units. County authorities, however, said his sizeable project demanded an EIS. Undaunted, Peterson expressed optimism, saying that local schools were under capacity, removing the usual objection to large developments. No dispute existed on that point; the district had surplused several schools because of a sharp decline in enrollment. Peterson also argued that a shortage of apartments existed, another good omen for his $15 million project.

Peterson hadn't reckoned with the Zenith Coalition, however. His permit application gave birth to the coalition, an ad hoc, unincorporated group representing citizens in several neighborhoods surrounding the vacant site. They had about six months to prepare for the EIS hearing, unlike the year involved in the Hidden Harbor saga. In a way, they only had a month, because the county issued the draft EIS on October 5, then held the hearing on November 2, 1978.

Here are the highlights of the step-by-step work that preceded the hearing. Coalition members:

1. Researched the zoning history of the site, finding a disparity that resembled a defect (the developer wanted apartment use, but the old rezone was for retirement-home use)
2. Kept track of comments by old-timers who didn't object to the retirement-home rezone, thus indicating they weren't antidevelopment
3. Collected signatures on a petition
4. Requested an evening hearing in writing, in the hope of gaining a good turnout
5. Elicited letters from public and private authorities to strengthen coalition arguments on substantive issues like traffic and drainage
6. Sought information from staff (county traffic engineers and planners) on traffic and other substantive issues in the draft EIS
7. Conducted a housing survey on the number of new units, hoping to undermine the developer's argument on the need for housing
8. Pooled information at a prehearing study session
9. Alerted the community on the date, time, and place of the EIS hearing.

Core coalition members found staffers whose views coincided with their case, and they heeded suggestions about compiling evidence. Finding these staff sources in other counties means being alert to helpful suggestions when compiling data on traffic and other issues. In regard to internal communication, core coalition members relied on telephone calls, instead of community meetings; thus, in this case, there is simply less of a prehearing saga to recount. On the other hand, there is more to be learned from the hearing presentation. With the presentation, it is easy to see the homework behind each point made.

The coalition's request for an evening community hearing— instead of a daytime courthouse one—paid off when about 200 residents jammed a neighborhood school on November 2, 1978. A petition bearing 1,075 signatures was presented to hearing officials. Then the crowd heard the coalition's lawyer present essentially the information members had pooled several days before the hearing.

The first argument advanced, and demonstrated by coalition testimony, was that the coalition wasn't antidevelopment. Many landowners said that they did not object in 1968 when the Grand

Lodge of Free Accepted Masons won a rezone for 178 units to expand its retirement facility on the site that Peterson was buying for
Highland Village. That would not have changed the character of
their single-family neighborhood, they said. They did believe if the
Masons sold this still-vacant land to the Polygon Corporation, it
would adversely affect the neighborhood; transient units housing
1,316 people were considered far different from a retirement home.
To document this point, the coalition entered as an exhibit a June
23, 1968, newspaper article, to the effect that the 1968 rezone to
multi-units was for a particular and limited use—to expand the retirement home. To demonstrate further that actual use and occupancy would be changed, the coalition entered data on the number of
parking places at the existing Mason retirement home and two others
nearby. From three retirement homes, there were 60 autos; associated with Highland Village would be parking spaces for 2,000 autos.
Furthermore, coalition lawyer Clark Snure argued that zoning—when
used for apartment purposes—violated the County Comprehensive
Land-Use Plan, the Highline Communities Plan, and the city of Des
Moines Comprehensive Plan. (Des Moines is near the site.) Several policies from the Highline Communities Plan that were alleged-
ly violated were set forth. Remember, Snure reminded, county ordinance 3747 says that the community plan governs when there is a
conflict between existing zoning and the use specified in the community plan. Clearly, prehearing preparation involved study of
county land plans and policies.

Then Snure argued against perceived defects in the economic
impact section of the EIS. (This EIS section is like a checkbook: if
the project is built, $X in taxes generated will be deposited in the
county account, then $X will be withdrawn to pay for police, fire
protection, and other services.) Snure demanded revision and expansion of the EIS "checkbook" to include increased expense for fire
and police equipment, manpower, overhead, fringe benefits, employment taxes, office support staff, and maintenance and operation
of vehicles. Using a ratio of one firefighter per 25 new Highland
Villagers, Snure said 1,316 people means an increase of 53 calls
per year. Coalition members urged serious study of the financial
impact on taxpayers.

The coalition was equally precise on the economic impact of
traffic. Specifically, the coalition listed seven street locations that
would need upgrading. The county and state had not scheduled this
construction for before the anticipated completion date of Highland
Village, according to the coalition, nor had such construction been
funded. Citizens insisted that the developer help pay his way with
highway construction, signalization, and improvements.

The coalition lawyer took exception to EIS traffic statistics, noting that too many of them were based on 1976 statistics, others were done on a one- or two-day basis, and still others were undertaken on days when extenuating circumstances (bad weather, no school) minimized traffic. In particular, Snure dismissed the 6.5 trips per unit mentioned in the EIS, saying that the coalition had obtained updated rates from the county traffic engineer indicating 9 trips per day per unit. Snure urged EIS revisions. The EIS didn't take into account such variables as traffic from a nearby state waterfront park, a community college, and a marina, he said—nor did the incomplete picture in the EIS take into account traffic accidents from Des Moines police reports and fire department accident aid calls. Statistics were added, making the accident total zoom upward. High accident rates suggest too many drivers and/or not enough street improvements.

Then the coalition countered Peterson's plea of a shortage of apartments. Members inserted into the record their survey of residential units semicompleted or completed since 1977. Their survey was based on building-permit data (available at county building departments) and personal observation. How could the developer dispute a tally of 1,079 units, each listed by address? Residents didn't hesitate to point out the potential traffic impact from 1,079 units, plus traffic impact from projected college enrollment.

Homework was also evident when the coalition entered as exhibits the following letters. Members had contacted a variety of sources, asking for a written reply.

Community college letters, expressing concern about traffic problems in the Highland Village area nearby, plus data on the influx of student traffic

A county letter, saying that acquisition of the Highland Village site for a county park was a live issue, contrary to other impressions

A school district letter, responding to a coalition inquiry about the need for park facilities by pointing to the current shortage of soccer and other playfields. Minus the potential 30-acre park, plus the 1,316 newcomers, the park problem would be compounded, the coalition argued.

A civil engineer's letter, giving a technical analysis of water drainage problems. A resident of the area, he faulted the "poor quality" of the EIS drainage section and called for revisions.

Outside authority also came into play when the coalition cited court cases, including SAVE v. Bothell (see Chapter 9). This state Supreme Court ruling holds that impact on an entire area must be

considered in making a land-use decision. The city of Des Moines
was neither consulted nor considered, the Des Moines mayor testified. This ally said 646 units would strain services, and that the
city had been preparing to annex the area.

In asking the county to deny the permit, the coalition also cited
county ordinance 3821. It provides that the county's policy is to approve, deny, or condition all private proposals so as to mitigate or
prevent identified significant adverse environmental impacts.

Sand subsequently rejected the building permit, based on ordinance 3821 and on a wide range of adverse impacts. The 646-unit
apartment would overload roads, strain fire protection, and invite
future zoning changes, Sand said. The added public costs for fire
service would be three times the revenues to the district, he said,
adding that such a financial impact could not be mitigated, with likely results being reduced fire safety for others. Thus, the county
denied the permit on March 20, 1979, making this the first time it
had taken such action under provisions of the State Environmental
Policy Act of 1971.

From the beginning, the Zenith Coalition demonstrated what
every land-use player must do: concentrate on collecting evidence.
These protesters didn't stop with dissecting the draft EIS and attempting to reduce the developer's credibility by pointing out inac-
curacies and oversights. They went on to the next step when they
submitted data (such as letters, a building permit survey, and traffic information), striving to refute his claims. Those data wouldn't
have been collected if the residents had not established good relations with staff members; their voice wouldn't have been as strong
if the Des Moines mayor hadn't stepped forth to testify. Organiza-
tionally, Highland Village and Hidden Harbor resisters did the right
thing by decentralizing, distributing the work among several members. Unlike Hidden Harbor residents, the Zenith Coalition decided
to forsake community meetings generally, feeling they are a waste
of time. The lesson to be drawn is that leaders must evaluate their
own individual situation. Some neighbors want rallies and coffee
klatches; others don't. The main point is that both groups effectively mobilized people power. Highland Village protesters avoided
missteps: they could have failed to ask for an EIS hearing, and gotten none; they could have missed asking for an evening community
hearing and had a sparse turnout at the courthouse in the daytime;
and they could have failed to turn in a written account of verbal testimony. They chose instead to ensure their input by turning in a
19-page written summary.

IN A NUTSHELL

Hidden Harbor and Highland Village protesters applied the following advice from Hillis, Aramburu, Webb, and others almost perfectly:

1. Embark on hearing preparation early.
2. Build a strong case.
3. Seek information from staff members.
4. Use courtesy.
5. Give a concise hearing presentation.
6. Encourage allies to testify in your favor.

When these two groups built strong cases, they assured the county that it could deny a building permit and withstand a court test. Their research armed the county with a strong potential defense. For example, how could the Hidden Harbor developer argue that services were adequate when the water district letter was evidence to the contrary? In both cases, residents presented the wheat of evidence, not the superfluous chaff. They organized themselves before the hearing, thus avoiding repetitious testimony. They must have known— to use Aramburu's phrase—that officials would rather be home watching television. They "slipped on the system's shoes," and succeeded.

DEFUSING THE DYNAMITE

Friction is a constant theme in this chapter, beginning with people who "go bananas" and "come to the hearing with their guns oiled." Hillis, Webb, and Aramburu made moves to minimize friction. The county can mandate an EIS to head off the friction of a court suit from protesters; it can issue building permits when adverse impact is hazy to sidestep court suits from developers. All of this raises the question of whether friction is worse than it needs to be and whether basic changes are in order. Hillis advocated some basic changes when he examined the anatomy of friction.

Misperception creates friction, he said, sharply criticizing press reports that "tend to reinforce people's perceptions. When the press says, 'The developers want to pave over Soos Creek—the residents want to preserve it,' the developer is getting a bum break." Hillis represented Soos Creek developers. Instead of the bad guy-good guy angle, he asked, why not examine the issues of when and to what extent should growth be allowed, and what mechanism should be used for allowing desired growth.

He holds similarly strong feelings about the friction he finds the county creating. "The policy of elected officials is not being carried out," Hillis charged. "A lot of staff members run off, making recommendations, contrary to county policy. The Building and Land Development Division and the county are in a head-on confrontation. It's an absolutely incredible waste of taxpayer dollars. The only thing [plan, policy] that we have is what the county formally adopted in writing. Until the thing is changed, they should stick with it." Hillis maintained that this independence throws "a monkey wrench" into the "certainty" or predictability needed. (Ed Sand, division director, countered that the division tries to make recommendations based on adopted plans and ordinances. Maybe Hillis was talking about recommendations on pending ordinances, pending community plans, or "red flagging," Sand said. He added that red flagging means the division tells the council whenever an application for a rezone or other ruling is inconsistent with a community plan not yet adopted by the council.)

One of the real problems is a lack of understanding of what land use is all about, Hillis explained. Hillis felt the problem exists not just with the average citizen, but with large property owners, developers, real-estate agents, elected officials, planners, and news reporters. Everyone voices the same frustrations, he said, adding that frustrations come from an inability to predict what concerns are going to be tomorrow. Land plans are going to be out-of-date tomorrow; but nobody is willing to acknowledge that today, Hillis asserted.

His remedy includes convincing people that plans aren't cast in concrete and devising an orderly system of change. One way of convincing people is to discard the system whereby well-intentioned planners advocate colors on a map. Currently, land-use maps are printed with yellow, for example, over all single-family zone areas, and another color over commercial zone areas, and various colors for other zoning classifications. People believe colors indicate all industrial or apartment use, Hillis explained. This adds needless friction, he added. Instead, the county should go toward policy, criteria, and standards, he urged. For instance, if people want multi-units only adjacent to arterial roads and commercial zoning, that idea could become policy. Ideally, he explained, the county council should formulate guiding principles. The citizens could use those principles as a springboard to what they want. Then the council could heed their voices in establishing refined standards.

Indeed, some changes in the county process are overdue. Those who want to defuse the dynamite ask, Why not make change so people don't "go bananas"? Why not make change so people don't come to the hearing "with their guns oiled"? In particular, why not correct a 1968 rezone "mistake" before the developer wastes $7,000 on a Hidden Harbor EIS, and before the neighbors waste legal fees, energy, and emotion?

5

FIFTY TIPS

Campaigns on land use are never easy, but tips collected from veteran campaigners, lawyers, and officials can prevent pitfalls. Here is a synopsis of their ideas, organized into four sections. The first section arms developers and protesters with an insider's knowledge on how the Environmental Impact Statement (EIS) process really works. Land-use players can learn how to crack the EIS code and how to save money on EIS appeals. The second section gives a glimpse into how lawmakers operate. Those who fail to learn from these behind-the-scenes insights gamble with losing. Then the third section gives a brief primer on rezone and other hearings. Reading the first and third sections is essential, since insights gleaned from the experts apply in both cases. In the fourth section, the serious student will find out how to work long range.

ENVIRONMENTAL IMPACT STATEMENTS

Preview the EIS process. It begins with staff evaluation of the environmental check list supplied by the developer. A declaration of nonsignificance means no EIS is necessary; a declaration of significance calls for an EIS. Subsequently, the developer submits a draft to the city or county, which is the ultimate "author." Issuance of a draft EIS triggers a 35-day public-comment period. A hearing may or may not be held. Then a final EIS is released, followed by 7 days for comment. The decision—perhaps for the building permit—is announced after the 7 days have elapsed. (Turn to Appendix E for more, including excerpts from an actual EIS.)

Canvass the neighborhood with a carefully drawn statement, especially if you are a protester. Be specific about objections and about whatever is requested. Developers should elicit letters or petitions of support too, perhaps from the local chamber of commerce.

Always ask for a hearing on Environmental Impact Statements. Members of one citizen group had to retrace their steps, door to door, because their first petition didn't ask for a hearing. Requests, in a petition or letter, should be submitted to the county building and land development division director or the director's counterpart in other jurisdictions. A written request should be made for a community hearing in the evening, instead of the customary courthouse one in the daytime, to encourage maximum turnout of citizens.

Send well-reasoned letters to the county executive, the county councilman or councilwoman representing your district, the department of planning and community development director, and the building and land development division director (BALD), as well as to staffers assigned to the case. Use the county's file number (or building permit application number) when you call BALD to pinpoint staff names. A massive outpouring of mail isn't incorporated into the draft EIS, but you should request that particularly well-researched letters be incorporated into the draft EIS. The county executive's infrequent statements sometimes demonstrate a principle—such as that community plans, not sewer districts, should dictate growth. Does your case demonstrate a principle?

Expand your voice by including letters from interested parties. A developer may include a letter elicited from a sewer district, stating that sewer service is sufficient to serve the building. On the other hand, a mayor of a nearby city may be glad to write, if asked, about the city's objections to traffic fall-out.

Be forewarned that winning is an uphill fight when the developer already has appropriate zoning. Such zoning gives the developer certain private-property rights.

Don't lump all developers into one package. One successful developer extraordinaire truly loves the land, winning environmental awards for his buildings. Another insults the land.

Learn about water run-off if you intend to stay in the development business. Early in the game, find out how to design a development to diminish run-off problems, and how to install precautionary measures. Bales of hay, for example, will slow down run-off. Residents should learn about run-off, even though it's not a sexy topic. Its ways become wanton when a developer denudes the landscape, eliminating nature's absorption through vegetation. Parking lots intensify unruliness. Improper treatment floods basements and yards and sends walls of mud slipping onto adjoining property. In one case, Orville Fischer of Everett recovered $11,800 in damages in a court suit over water run-off. (Note: Residents should be aware of nearby springs, septic-tank drainage, soil composition, and signs of erosion. Inform authorities about problems, especially through EIS documents. Free advice from staff members is valuable.)

Maintain contact with your counterparts in other disputes. Ask if they know a county planner or engineer whose planning views coincide with your case.

Inspect EIS reports at the public library, city hall, or county courthouse for ideas. One EIS documented that suburban developments generate a higher level of traffic than do urban developments, contrary to data in many EIS reports.

Xerox the list of names and agencies to which the EIS was sent for review. This cuts red tape and helps in compiling a guest list for a community meeting. On the other hand, this list cues the developer in on whom to contact early on for reaction.

Study the developer's EIS draft at the courthouse, challenging figures or descriptions for accuracy—or insert items the developer may have intentionally overlooked. Written comments may be submitted to the county environmental specialist. The draft leading to the second draft EIS is not a secret document, contrary to the belief of some residents.

Check with the National Oceanic and Atmospheric Administration (local offices are listed in the telephone book under U.S. Government) for weather conditions on the day the traffic count was taken, to detect if the developer gave a count from a day constrained by snowy or wet weather. Counter with rush-hour figures counted by volunteers.

Use a curious mind. Is the project in compliance with the map and intent of the community land-use plan? Will it overextend the water or fire district? Will water run-off damage adjoining property or streams? Is the traffic count current? Does it take

into account parent chauffeurs who descend en masse on Little
League ballfields ?

Head off hearing trouble, if you are a developer, by not leaving the foregoing flaws in the EIS. Furthermore, if the project
poses a traffic hazard, negotiate remedies with authorities at the
onset. In one case, traffic authorities installed a needed left-turn
channelization, averting an outcry from protesters.

Present verbal and written testimony at the EIS hearing, if
you won one.

Trim court expense in EIS appeals by using the little-known
alternative of a rehearing. ("If BALD allows a building permit on
the basis of EIS information, or imposes conditions, you can appeal
to the zoning examiner," explained Robert Johns, a county prosecutor. The examiner gives the final decision on a permit and
makes a recommendation to the council on rezones and subdivisions.
Decisions may be appealed to the court.)

Learn the lingo of the shoreline law, if applicable. Shoreline
protection ranges from oil port facilities down to such small-scale
matters as the violation for which a Wenatchee River man was cited
when he dumped debris into the river. (In Washington State, for
example, there are governing bodies for variances and conditional-
use permits. Exemptions may be sought. To broaden understanding of the Shoreline Management Act of 1971, read R.C.W. 90.58
and WAC 173-14. R.C.W., the revised code of Washington, means
state law; WACs are agency regulations.) Weyerhaeuser officials
are probably aware of the shoreline law, having spent more than
$3 million in studies, planning, and legal fees in attempting to make
a Nisqually delta export complex a reality. The act singles out the
Nisqually delta as an environmentally sensitive area that needs
special protection. Weyerhaeuser encountered resistance from
local environmentalists. (In regard to the shoreline law: one developer said that he uses an 18-inch culvert to determine if flow in
a body of water is 20 cubic feet per second.)

LAWMAKERS

Learn about council dynamics. A five-to-four split was characteristic. One of the five was Mike Lowry, who quit the courthouse for a seat in Congress, much to the regret of many protesters.
Another of the bloc of five was Bernice Stern, who subsequently
retired from the council. Stern said that many times a commercial
developer who has not met all council criteria manages to get in.

Display widespread support for more impact than a one-on-
one visit. If one individual visits one decision maker, that person

may not win responsiveness. To display support, either send petitions or send a group to meet with the decision maker. Members of one group went to see a councilman who was unfriendly to their views. He reversed his position.

Remember that developers can exert the same kind of influence. Mr. Big Shot shows up at a hearing with a battery of architects, lawyers, and assistants. "His suit costs three times as much as suits worn by the officials. They reason he must be right, he's made so much money," commented an inside observer, concluding that Mr. Big Shot won.

Heed the way that old war stories portray obstacles. In a Renton case, two suburban councilmen were reluctant to kill a rezone, saying that it would only increase pressure for development in their districts. Their districts already suffered from traffic congestion, they retorted. Similar dynamics occur as King County reacts to the new Snohomish County fee structure (see Part I, Chapter 1) since fees may drive developers to King County, according to observers.

Know that certain council members don't have the vaguest notion of where the property at issue is located. Use graphic maps or photographs to clue them in quickly. Confusion is your worst enemy. Give a concise presentation.

Keep in mind that staffers can be overworked, giving them insufficient time to examine the case. Enter the developer's skillful lawyer. Zap. You lose.

Bear in mind the outrage of two veteran protest leaders over the attitude of officialdom. Carol Berwald and Luella Gestner found some officials uninterested in citizens. They pointed out that officials abruptly became attentive when land-use lawyer Roger Leed came on the scene—officials didn't want to tangle with Leed or a possible legal challenge.

Obtain a list of local officials from the state association of counties and state association of cities. This list is a good memory aid.

HEARINGS

Present facts. Never unleash a stormy tirade before any official. Let the other guy get mad.

Work early on. You'll be more effective at the hearing. Lawyer Peter Buck advised developer clients to get a comprehensive plan map and text at the onset. You may almost have to force your way into planning departments, he said, because they're trying to save you money, but insist on the whole map and text. In

reference to the prehearing report he said that, if you can do it
without being pushy, you can write the draft recommendations for
the planners on the project. Furthermore, he feels it is advisable
to submit a rational letter to decision makers a week before the
hearing. Your opinion loses effectiveness when presented only at a
hearing, he added.

Seek wisdom from veteran campaigners. Veteran developers
use data on the shortage of housing or rentals to argue for their
subdivision or condominiums. Data may be obtained from the planning department or from private real-estate research organizations.
Veteran citizen campaigners use facts to argue against a disproportionate percentage of large-scale development in their community, thus avoiding being accused of an antidevelopment stance.

Do your homework. Compile a map on the number of units,
pending and recently approved, to show the accumulative impact on
roads. Use the map to enlist allies in the neighborhood and to in-
form decision makers, before the hearing and during the hearing.
Most are surprised at what's going on. You haven't argued against
development—but you've planted a seed of doubt in decision makers'
minds. You've stimulated their questions on whether the roads
can handle the influx. Homework begins when you gather data from
neighborhood and county sources (some county planners don't know
about rezone applications up the street). Pinpoint each project on
the map with a number; next to a corresponding number below, list
the number of units and the status of the project, including the time,
place, and date of coming hearings.

Voice feelings by public-opinion telegram, sometimes avail-
able from Western Union at a lower rate than a regular telegram.
Telegrams should be supplemented by detailed, documented letters.
Each serves a purpose.

Beat the knowledge gap. Few know that the county zoning
code can be inspected in local libraries, or that the county maintains a land-use library in the courthouse. Attend other land-use
hearings to learn the ropes; strike up a conversation with other
protesters. Developers who don't attend hearings for training are
courting trouble.

Use tools of the development trade with caution. Each page
of the Metzger Map depicts one township and shows rivers, county
lines, and roads. Don't rely on ownership identification, though;
check with the title company or assessor's office for current
ownership. There are counterparts to the Metzger and Thomas
Brothers' maps in other jurisdictions. More universal is a Kroll
Map, showing sections, roads, and so on. Citizens may inspect
the Kroll Map at the assessor's office. Another tool is a soils
survey map, available from the U.S. Department of Agriculture.
It may or may not be accurate.

Bear in mind that the owner's name is critical because she or he could be a campaign contributor of officials who decide the case, creating a conflict of interest. For public records of contributors, contact the Public Disclosure Commission in Olympia (or its counterpart in other states) or the county records and elections division. Some businesses disguise contributions by using names of employees. One group examined a councilman's election letterhead stationery, discovering the developer listed with loyalists.

Combat coy owner-applicants who go by dummy company names. Outfoxed You Inc. or C.O.N.C.E.A.L. Co.? Not quite, but some phantom company names are put-ons. Laws in many states require firms to register officers. Check for officers' names with the secretary of state or corresponding official in your state. Another tactic is to inspect tax records on file with the county assessor, which give the owner's name and address. Save time by bringing a legal description of the property, if available, to the assessor's office. (That address, in one case, was the only clue. Tax records merely listed the name of the corporation, which the developer had created for that property; nor was the developer listed on building-permit applications, although the forms were properly signed by his architect and contractor. Going to the address on the tax records revealed his identity.)

Investigate who has an option to buy, as well as who owns the land in question. This knowledge helps to evaluate the developer's strategy and to predict the shabbiness or nonshabbiness of the building, which can have an impact on property taxes. A local developer might yield to pressure and withdraw his or her plans, advised Jim Lemen, whose group rebuffed the 646-unit Highland Village. Canadians and other foreigners care less, he added, and their influx should be dealt with by legislation prohibiting foreign speculators. Although voters defeated a state measure against foreign speculators years ago, the issue hasn't been dead in Olympia.

Copy down the fact that there are 43,560 square feet per acre.

Park free in the county parking building, available in some jurisdictions, while attending the hearing. Inquire in advance whether free public parking is available by the courthouse or county administrative building. Watch the two-hour time limit.

Rally peacefully, if you decide to hold a rally. Monitors should be appointed to maintain order and to prevent altercations between bystanders and participants. Ask whether the American Friends Service Committee will provide monitors, for payment of a sum to cover costs. If you use the streets, you must obtain a parade permit in some jurisdictions. To apply for a permit, prepare a fact sheet describing the date, route, issue, sponsoring organization, address, and phone, to deliver to the appropriate government office.

Bear this axiom in mind: put it in writing. Then you won't suffer the fate of a crowd of 900 that resisted area-wide zoning changes involving almost 2,000 acres of property. Hearing testimony seemed to fall on open ears. County officials reassured the tearful, joked with others, and extended personal hellos to members of the stormy crowd. Few points were scored by the process. A citizen activist later discovered that verbal testimony—without submission of written testimony—would not be considered; but the need to "put it in writing" was never announced at the meeting.

Avert awkwardness before decision makers. Lawyer Tom Goeltz advises early inquiry about suspected violations of the Appearance of Fairness Doctrine. Write to the prosecutor or city attorney, stating that, "We understand that Mr. X and Councilman X have. . . ." Prehearing exchanges are forbidden by the Appearance of Fairness Doctrine in Washington State. Goeltz, a former deputy prosecutor, specializes in land use.

Ask for reconsideration of judgments made by the zoning examiner when you have grounds for the request. Take heart from the success of Sharon Bernhardt, who secured a rezone modification when an office building was approved for her Riverton neighborhood.

Beware of changes after hearing decisions. (If you're a developer, try this tactic.) One group discovered that the losing developer reapplied, asking for fewer units per acre. He won the second time around.

LONG-RANGE STRATEGY

Work long range by establishing real-estate covenants (agreements between neighbors)—for example, to forbid neighbors from blocking the view.

Be alert to community planning. Provide written input into community plans being formed. Keep a close watch on "area zoning"—when existing zoning is brought into closer compliance with community plans. It can translate into an infusion of apartments. It has downzoned land (for example, from multi-unit to residential use), causing cries of "being robbed of property value." The only legal requirement for public notice of a hearing on rezoning hundreds of individual properties came because the county council's area-zoning action was by ordinance, which demands notice, according to a planner. Don't let changes in the city or county comprehensive land-use plan or zoning code slip by, either. Both are crucial.

Convert sites that are a thorn in the side of the community into parks. The county park division buys park sites. The Hidden Harbor Motel developer, for one, offered to sell part of his site in the county (see Part II, Chapter 4). In addition, the Nature Conservancy, Seattle, buys land to retain permanently or to transfer to the government. Agencies reimburse the conservancy. The Washington Parks Foundation, Seattle, accepts donations and can turn land over to agencies. The owner who donated $120,000 of Green River land for a park provided a classic case of how an owner can benefit from an income-tax break by donating land.

Ponder the words of Stanley Hallet, president of Woodstock Institute, which works on Chicago urban problems. Chicago has a $1 billion sewer tunnel, he said. Instead of blowing that money, he asked, why not recycle organic waste closer to its source? Instead of elaborate water run-off controls, why not slow water run-off with porous paving and with berms at the source? Hallet is a lecturer at the graduate school of management at Northwestern University and is board chairman of a computer firm.

Exert muscle effectively. One real-estate crowd of almost 100 went to the state capital to convey feelings to lawmakers; but they didn't know the mechanics of staging a demonstration. Learn a lesson from their inexperience. For impact, prearrange an introduction from House and Senate leaders before the troops are marshaled in the Capitol building. Ask the doormen at the House and Senate side of Capitol chambers to transmit your note ("Please introduce our delegation in the north gallery—the State Association of _____. We'll be in the gallery at 10:30 A.M. today. Thank you, John Doe, President") to the legislator in charge. Wear something, perhaps red jackets, so lawmakers can readily observe group strength when you're sitting up in the visitors' gallery. Finally, coach members to stand up in a bloc upon introduction by House and Senate leaders. (Much of the real-estate crowd did wear red jackets; they also caught on quickly to the mechanics of a demonstration.) Then, when lawmakers leave the main chambers, constituents from their districts should stop by their offices or meeting rooms (pre- or postmeeting) to bend their ear briefly. The same principles apply at the council and commission level; let them know you're from their district.

Shave costs by incorporating as a nonprofit group: lawyers may give free time because state bar association ethics recommend devoting a certain amount of time to public service. Instructions on incorporating are available in Incorporation and Business Guide for Washington, by Harold Coe. However, some groups dismiss the incorporation structure, feeling it entails too much time and money (mainly, $100 to file with the secretary of state). Lawyers disagree on whether incorporating protects against lawsuits. From the consumer's viewpoint, one incentive for incorporation is the tax advantage. Donations to a group that qualifies as nonprofit are deductible. So save those canceled checks.

Watch Washington State, California, Colorado, Connecticut, and Florida to see what's coming in the years ahead. Yankelovic, Shelly and White, a polling/market forecasting firm based in Washington, D.C., has concluded that social and governmental trends in these states have been bellwethers for the rest of the country. Trends that the firm now sees are greater electorate involvement in real-estate development and environmental issues; increasing use of initiatives and referendums to regulate real-estate development; decentralization of power and institutions; and fiscal conservatism.

6

AN AGENCY YOUR ANATHEMA?
HOW TO TOPPLE A TITAN

Criminals wind up on the "most wanted" list. Not so with the prisons that hold them. Pam Williams and her neighbors resisted a 500-man prison, proposed for their backyards. Finally, the state relented. Dixy Lee Ray then governor, announced that the state would not pursue those sites, thus amazing political pundits. Then the mighty state Department of Social and Health Services (DSHS) backed down from the two Tacoma sites.

How did David bring down Goliath? Actually, the techniques used were nothing more than the tactics employed by adept home-owners fighting a neighborhood developer: research, factual argu-ment, allies, the positive approach, and the squeaky-wheel tech-nique. All these techniques are used against the titans—the ports and nuclear and oil pipeline monoliths.

In this case, the state's initial strategy was revealed October 15, 1979, when DSHS announced two site proposals. "I found out about it on the news," said a surprised state Representative George Walk, a Democrat representing the area. Apparently DSHS did not confer in advance with local officials.

Angry residents flooded Walk and other officials with protest calls, giving them an earful. "Immediate resistance began," said Williams, a teacher. "Our South Hill Puyallup Community united first through a PTA meeting. After conferring with a lawyer, we held a meeting which drew close to 1,000 residents."

Immediate discouragement also began. A DSHS official, Robert Kastama, informed residents that resistance would have no effect on the outcome. "DSHS has a flagrant disregard for local at-titude," Walk declared, echoing legislators who label DSHS "arro-gant." "Wisely, protesters avoided a head-on scrap with DSHS," observed a lawyer close to the struggle. "Instead, they employed a political strategy." They forged a political partnership.

"Representative Dan Grimm taught us how to lobby; Representative Phillis Erickson provided some much needed research; and Walk got a seat on the Institutions Committee, strengthening his voice on jail siting," Williams explained. In turn, Walk said, "We used information from the homeowners' research committee for talks with fellow legislators. For instance, the committee told us specifically how the prison would adversely impact the whole community. Overall, we stressed that both sites were bad for any development. We used a constructive, positive approach. It wasn't a matter of people being scared of a prison. Instead, we spoke of a better alternative. McNeil Island is a popular alternative with lawmakers." There was a move to turn the soon-to-be-abandoned federal prison over to the state. Only Governor Ray, whose home is near McNeil, dismissed McNeil as unacceptable.

Undeterred, residents mobilized. One team called all the numbers in the Tacoma vicinity's telephone book to enlist support. "We passed out pamphlets and sold T-shirts," Williams continued. "Citizens Against Prison On South Hill" was imprinted on T-shirts; T-shirts and bumper stickers enrich campaign coffers and create visibility. ("Shed A Northern Tier," imprinted on anti-Northern Tier Pipeline T-shirts, proved an eyecatcher in a different campaign.)

Support coalesced. On the eve of the legislative session, 100 homeowners sent 100 letters to each member of the Institutions and Appropriations Committees. The Appropriations Committee recommends funding for prisons. "I'm getting writer's cramp," a weary Williams said when she finished her hand-written letters.

Prison opponents spoke and wrote knowledgeably, both to elected officials and to DSHS, because they had done their homework. Working with their lawyer, residents had researched potential impact on traffic, water supply and run-off, flood control, and percolation (the soil's ability to handle septic tanks). They discovered DSHS quoted outdated maps; in one case, DSHS used a 30-year-old map to rate water supply adequate. The old map indicated aquifers were adequate to support wells.

DSHS, like other agencies, had also compiled criteria for site selection. "But DSHS criteria had a lot of flaws," Walk said. "We went over DSHS site-selection criteria with a fine-tooth comb," Williams added. "Using DSHS facts and figures, we came up with very different conclusions."

Logic dictates that DSHS would select sites with the highest number of points on the scale of criteria. "But they didn't even pick the sites with the highest points," Walk said, complaining of the

Tacoma selections from the list of 200 sites. "The main reason our site was unsuitable was that the state had no legal access to the site," Williams pointed out. "No owner would give the state permission to cross their land to the landlocked prison site." She calculated that this would delay the project.

Facts, not emotionalism, were the key to success. For example, opponents stressed that the state could save tax money by using a site next to the existing Monroe prison. Services could be shared.

When Governor Ray abandoned the Tacoma sites, she announced the Monroe site. Outrage erupted in Monroe, and a replay unfolded. Local officials, caught by surprise by news broadcasts, complained bitterly that the 500-man prison would overload utilities and government services. "The state failed to consult with us," they complained.

Residents organized, pledging to bring political pressure to bear. The Skykomish Valley Improvement Association retained lawyer Roger Leed, who prepared to argue that the Monroe selection was "arbitrary and capricious," and therefore illegal.

DSHS, however, rallied a proprison band of residents. Gerald Thompson, then DSHS chief, admitted at a community meeting that his agency had quietly drawn up plans to organize a group of residents to speak out in support of the 500-bed prison. "You organize and we do it, too," Thompson retorted—and so it goes.

The Monroe protest may not be as successful as the Tacoma drive. Tacoma's timing was ideal: it was election year for the governor and for most legislators. (Incidentally, Ray lost.) Tacoma stalwarts were also fortunate to have the services of lawyer Gary Weber. "Weber has been super, donating countless hours," Williams recalled.

Other citizen campaigns can't afford a lawyer; they can't afford to incur legal bills beyond their modest means. By contrast, the government has "free" legal service. The prosecutor, the state attorney general, and port lawyers supply legal counsel. Of course, it's not really free, for taxpayers ultimately foot the bill.

Time and again, citizens complain of this disadvantage. This restriction restrains citizen combatants, they say. Only the affluent, like a Normandy Park community that spent $15,000 to win a suit against the government, can afford to challenge the government.

One group works to correct the imbalance. "1,000 Friends provides attorneys at no cost when questions involve issues of statewide importance," said Henry Richmond, executive director of the Oregon citizen group. (Members of 1,000 Friends make pledges, typically $100 per year, to support the group. Less support comes from grants.) "We also provide attorneys to ensure that local officials comply with the Oregon Land Conservation and Development Commission's (LCDC) goals. Any new body of law presents questions of interpretation which courts must resolve. Oregon's land-use laws—aimed at benefiting the public generally—are no exception. But who can afford $10,000 or more in attorney's fees?" The answer: few.

Legal legwork paid off with these court victories:

1,000 Friends won an appeal on behalf of Coos County citizens who charged that the county violated LCDC's citizen-involvement goal when it adopted the comprehensive land plan at a "special" meeting for which no notice was given and that no citizens attended. LCDC demanded that the county revise its citizen-involvement program. This case is known as League of Women Voters vs. Coos County.

1,000 Friends won a Circuit Court ruling that a city may not approve a subdivision without giving schools and special districts an opportunity to review the proposal and comment on impacts on the districts. This case is called Bientz v. the city of Dayton.

1,000 Friends successfully argued in the Oregon Supreme Court that the findings of fact required to support local land-use decisions—that is, the evidence relied on to show that applicable standards have been met—must be precise and carefully detailed, and "must explain why those facts lead [the local planning body] to make the decisions it makes." This was the Green v. Hayward case.

1,000 Friends established precedent in the Oregon Supreme Court and Court of Appeals: now LCDC goals must apply to city annexations, instead of only to rezone actions (Petersen v. Klamath Falls) and subdivisions (1,000 Friends v. Benton County).

"1,000 Friends is responsible for nearly all the major land-use rulings to come from the courts and LCDC in the past three years," Richmond observed. Vigilant, 1,000 Friends also monitors government land-use action. For example, the group conducted a six-month study of 69 sewer systems proposed for Oregon Department of Environmental Quality (DEQ) funding. The study identified major inconsistencies with LCDC sprawl-control standards, and 1,000 Friends successfully urged DEQ to adopt procedures ensuring coordination with LCDC.

1,000 Friends' victories testify that citizens can enjoy certain advantages. The prison fight, however, better illustrates those advantages. In the prison conflict, citizens received free help from legislators, reaped the results of zeal, and carried clout as voters.

On the other hand, government may work under one handicap. In the Normandy Park case, a citizen leader concluded that government research and legal representation were so sloppy that they left government vulnerable to defeat. Dee Pedersen, a League of Women Voters' activist who lives in Normandy Park, said that the government workers involved in the case "put in their time, but not their hearts."

LOOKING TO THE PUBLIC PURSE
FOR LOW-INTEREST LOANS

It's timely to examine the citizen versus government clash, because there is a trend toward public-private development. Public and private sectors are increasingly working together to pursue financing and permits for projects. Here are some actual examples, demonstrating the range of the "super developer":

A city or county housing authority builds and operates housing, in conjunction with a private firm or firms.

A church, teacher union, or other nonprofit organization wins federal funding of retirement homes, plus rent subsidies. HUD grants loans under Section 202 of the National Housing Program and subsidizes rents under the Section 8 Program. In one year alone, Catholic sponsors received 15 percent of the total loans, according to Timothy McInerney, Long Island editor of a builder's association publication. HUD loaned Catholic sponsors $75 million, at low interest rates, for housing for the elderly, McInerney said. "There is no substance to the contention that 'this is a violation of church and state principles' because no consideration of religion can be given in tenant selection," he added.

A private developer builds a chain store, supermarket, or office, thanks to low-interest special-revenue bonds obtained through the government.

A port authority acts as the real-estate landlord for holdings around an airport, and builds and operates marinas and more.

A federal agency—HUD—funds rehabilitation and construction of housing for the private sector.

A city or county applies for an Urban Development Action Grant (UDAG) for financing part of a private development.

One UDAG application cast Mayor Charles Royer in the role of a promoter for a Weyerhaeuser-subsidiary project when he went to Washington, D.C., for UDAG funding. As with "free" legal representation, private interests enjoyed free lobbying. The federal

funds sought came to $12 million, which was to be combined with
$93 million in private funds to build a five-block development, in-
cluding office and retail space. Weyerhaeuser switched the housing
element to condos when the government turned the application down,
reportedly only because the city had used up its share of UDAG.

The following case illustrates how developers can jump on the
public-private bandwagon in another way. Taking a cue from Min-
neapolis, the Downtown Seattle Development Association, Seattle
Master Builders, unions, bankers, realtors, and others initiated a
nonprofit corporation, aimed at developing "affordable" housing.
The group planned to ask the city to assign all available federal and
local funds for the housing program. Group plans were also brew-
ing for a public-bond issue to produce $12.5 million for five years
to finance the proposed housing construction.

One way private developers gain access to bond issues is
through special-revenue bonds. Put simply, the government applies
for a loan from the private money market. Loan proceeds go to private interests. Ultimately, money generated by the shopping center, hotel, or franchise repays the loan.

"What's the advantage? Three interest points," said Joel
Haggard, a lawyer who represents developers. Interest could drop
from 11 to 8 percent, or from 20 to 17 percent, depending on the
market, according to Haggard. By dropping three interest points,
"a borrower could save $70,000 per year on a $5 million bond,"
added Stan Finkelstein of the State Association of Cities. The association submitted a draft bill permitting revenue bonds to the legislature. "A grocery purchaser could pay $2.70 less per $100 of
groceries in a shopping center financed this way," Haggard contended (he assumes developers will pass the savings on to con-
sumers).

"Proponents cite Oregon as an example of how special-revenue
financing has succeeded," observed Brian K. Teller, vice-president
of the State Research Council. "In 1979 alone, Oregon approved
eligibility for more than $56 million in industrial-revenue bonds for
projects expected to add 3,300 jobs." Oregon started the program
in 1975.

Despite enthusiasm, marriages of public and private sectors
hit rocky roads. "Subsidy!" critics charge. "Yankee ingenuity!"
backers retort. "Government should not be in the business of fis-
cally upholstering business. Bonds only promote marginal enter-
prises," declared John Fluke of John Fluke Manufacturing Co.,
Everett.

Four New York assemblymen filed suit against the finance plan
for the 12-story American Stock Exchange Building. "Should New
York taxpayers subsidize new headquarters for the American Stock

Exchange? We don't think so." Thus read the headline emblazoned across the New York Public Interest Research Group (NYPIRG) publication. "Of the $53 million price tag on the new headquarters, taxpayers would be chipping in $20 million, through the state Urban Development Corporation. The Triborough Bridge and Tunnel Authority would issue bonds to raise the rest. . . . The American Stock Exchange would in turn lease the building from the two public authorities at a rental rate far below market value," NYPIRG's Citizen News stated. (It is now called Agenda for Citizen Involvement.)

The News scoffed at the American Stock Exchange—"citadel of the free enterprise system"—as "an unlikely candidate to get state aid." NYPIRG was a codefendant in the suit. "The suit charges that the plan is unconstitutional since it involves a 'loan or gift' from the state to a private corporation . . . and since it creates a debt on tax money without a public referendum," the News stated.

Constitutional objections to use of public funds for private purposes were also a consideration in legal challenges against a Eugene downtown development district. Oregon Supreme Court justices, however, held that the district was constitutional, as were taxes levied for its support.

Even the Washington State constitution, long the lone holdout against loaning the state's credit, is softening. Special-revenue bonds are permitted for certain purposes. Backers of bonds will lobby for an amendment to the state constitution, permitting revenue bonds in general.

Teller said that critics frequently pose the question, What is the effect on state or local bond ratings if an industrial-development bond issue defaults? Proponents, he continues, claim that bond holders will look to the credit of the facilities' users, not to the government.

Public-private marriages get too cozy, some critics charge. In one case, the wedding started when Portland planned to condemn four downtown blocks and make land available at reduced prices to a Canadian developer for hotel and retail development. The public purse would supply $19.5 million for land acquisition, clearance, and related improvements; proceeds from the Canadian purchaser would reduce the cost to taxpayers to $17.5 million, according to city consultant Don Barney. According to the Portland Development Commission, increased tax revenues would justify the $17.5 million expenditure. (The incentive for eloping, in many cases, is to give birth to a better tax base.)

"A special favor," scoffed a Williamette Week editorial. The editorial faulted "weak resolutions" by the city, which set "minimal conditions" on the project. "Capitulation," the editorial contended. Ultimately, the Cadillac Fairview developers withdrew the project, citing unfavorable economic conditions, Barney said.

"Capitulation," foes murmured again, on another project. This time HUD was resented, for having approved funding for a project that failed to meet HUD criteria. This $1.7 million, church-sponsored elderly complex was proposed for inappropriately zoned land and was two miles from shopping, local resident Ginger Babcock charged. She cited HUD criteria for proper zoning and nearby shopping.

Babcock and her band of neighbors discovered that HUD is an independent creature, unto itself, for HUD compiles and evaluates its own environmental check list, according to Richard Moore, HUD environmental officer. He was talking about funding of Section 8, 202, projects like the elderly complex.

Unlike some, complex proponent Jeanne Sack welcomes "a way to connect our religious energies to the government in a kind of a marriage." Sack sought a rezone and building permit for the yet-to-be-settled elderly project.

Zoltan Szigethy, Seattle Trust vice-president, speaks in general about what lies ahead. "There is a trend toward marriages," he predicted. "New cooperative mechanisms are created in the process, such as the Church Council's Common Ground and the business community's Housing Resources Group, both nonprofit housing development organizations that may in some ways compete for available public subsidies. Actions, such as Mayor Royer's proposal to pay for new housing for the elderly poor with revenue from a $55 million general-obligation bond, will proliferate."

There are at least two leaders who are worried about a proliferation of unchecked power. From today's experience, they know that checks need to be imposed on government. Even today, League of Women Voters' leader Pedersen and former Representative John Jovanovich, D-Seattle, work to instill a sense of responsibility. Independent entities, like the Port of Seattle, must be subject to county oversight on land use, they say. They find that the current lack of oversight lets the port expand, condemn, and develop at will. "The port is like having a black widow for a neighbor; you never know where and when it will jump," Pedersen said of port expansion.

Sitting near the pair at one of many legislative hearings on the port was Edward Marschall, who feels he is a victim of a $1.1 million port land grab. Marschall—like others who testified to no avail—wasn't always embittered at the port. In the 1930s, young Marschall came to this country with trust in his heart, grateful to escape arbitrary rule. Clearing his 15 acres for a farm, this immigrant had faith in his new country.

Today, he condemns the port for "illegally practicing condemnation when it confiscated my land, near Sea-Tac Airport." The port owns and runs the ever expanding airport. The port condemned his

15 acres in 1942, paying him $2,600, Marschall said, toting a brief-
case of records. It sold 10 acres for about $800,000 in 1972 to the
state Department of Highways, then traded off the remaining 5 acres,
amounting to a profit of $1,144,400 for the raw land, according to
the 65-year-old retiree. "The port shouldn't be allowed to turn condemned land for a huge profit," Marschall declared, his voice edged
with resentment. Moreover, "the port took my land for 'airport
purposes' when it should have had a 'comprehensive scheme for development' according to port bylaws."

In rebuttal, port general counsel Carol Doherty responded,
"There is no legal requirement for 'a comprehensive scheme.' However, as a matter of policy, the port in 1974 included airport properties within its Comprehensive Scheme of Harbor Improvements."

Marschall also felt the sting of injustice, he said, when the
port condemned his family home on three other acres in 1975. "We
lost $60,000 out of the $102,000 awarded to us by the jury because
we had to pay the attorney, appraiser, and court costs," he snapped.
Hundreds of others who formerly owned homes near the airport re-
late similar experiences.

Then there's Anthony Scherda, owner of nine acres for 50
years. Caught in government's response to growth patterns, he
shook his grey head in anguish when the government downzoned his
land. The county took that action to dampen growth in his area,
while it upzoned land in another area where it wanted to encourage
growth. And Howard Olson, 77, can't subdivide his own acre (half
occupied by his home) because the county thinks it might want his
land for future development and doesn't want to deal with two owners.

For Marschall, Scherda, and Olson, the government's appetite
for development evokes despair.

7

DEVELOPERS:
STRATEGIES FOR SUCCESS

John Miller planted the seeds of success long before his project won approval at the subdivision hearing. Like many developers, Miller bought land for his complex. Wisely, he avoided getting stuck with undevelopable land. In his earnest money,* Miller made the deal contingent upon obtaining subdivision and permit approval.

Then he applied in the name of the owner, a practice permitted in his jurisdiction. Miller suspected this tactic would elicit sympathy since the seller was a lone woman. This time, he didn't apply in the name of his architect, a respected figure.

---

*The meaning of the term "earnest money" is broad: (1) Earnest money is the money the purchaser gives the seller as part payment. As a pledge to purchase, it takes the property off the market. The purchaser may or may not lose the money by defaulting in the deal. (2) Colloquially, an earnest money contract may be called an earnest money. It actually is a short document that lists the amount of the earnest money partial payment; the purchase price and terms; the legal description of the property; and the amount of commission charged by the real-estate agent. It is an instrument that can contain conditions (known as clauses) that define the transaction and that can protect the buyer and seller. Clauses are added whenever it's O.K. with the buyer and seller—initially or later. As negotiations proceed, modifications (clauses) need to be initialed by the buyer and seller. The real-estate agent usually takes the contract from one party to the other, seeking signatures. Both the buyer and the seller must sign the contract before a deal is consummated.

Miller countered doubt, too. He knew the woman's worries were, "Did I get a good deal? Did I really do the right thing?" "You really got a good deal," Miller repeatedly reassured her. "I paid too much for your property." He defused more doubts with progress reports; he knew this would also reassure the seller.

Psychology paid off with the lender, as well. Miller avoided asking for a loan or an extension, knowing such a request would evoke a flat "no." Instead, he asked whether he could get a $225,000 or a $250,000 loan. "What are your terms for an extension of the loan we're discussing?" Miller asked, making it hard for the lender to say no to the loan request. Miller succeeded, with both the loan and the extension.

Over at the planning department, he obtained free information on prior decisions and pending zoning ordinances. He discovered one new ordinance for 5,000-square foot lots (instead of the old 7,200-square foot lots), allowing him four extra units. Smaller lots create higher density (units per acre). Courteous and credible, Miller won the respect of planners.

To win more friends, he pledged formation of an architectural board to ensure careful building practices. "Owners cherish their land," Miller observed. "I gained favor by naming the subdivision after the woman from whom the land was purchased."

However, some John Millers go broke. One such developer neglected to research the site's history—a legacy of government turndowns.

To save money, use this nuts-and-bolts check list. Arm yourself for a battle on several fronts: government, the citizenry, and the land itself.

WILL IT FLY?

Is the government decision-making body neutral; or is it dominated by progrowthers or antigrowthers? Let planners steer you to documents in earlier cases that reveal attitude, and investigate attitude by sitting in on hearings.

If a no-growth posture prevails, rethink plans, perhaps switching to property in a more receptive jurisdiction.

Also, inquire whether council or commission members are elected by district. Typically, your district's representative will have more interest in your project than nonrepresentatives will. Mull over whether to direct your selling campaign to him or her.

Research—on attitude and site location—will help you make decisions that will head off trouble from protesters.

PARACHUTING INTO A LANDLOCKED LOT?

Location, location, location: its importance cannot be over
emphasized. Inspect the property by walking the site. Search out
answers to the following questions:

1. Is it near eyesores or near farms that smell in the summer?
2. Does it have sufficient access? If it's landlocked (lacks access),
   you may fall prey to jokes about parachuting into the property.
3. Does the county or city public works department feel the main
   roads are overburdened? What road and sidewalk construction
   costs accrue to you? Are there any easements or restrictions
   on easements?
4. Would a location nearer public transportation lines improve selling price? Further, would it give you an argument about energy
   efficiency to use at the hearing?
5. What does your market analysis reveal about location when you
   inquire at the school district about schools for the offspring of
   buyers? If enrollment is declining, you have a ready-made hearing argument about helping to use underutilized facilities.
6. What does the actual development pattern indicate when examined
   in light of the proposed use? How can you use your conclusions
   to your advantage at a future hearing?

Beyond those matters, guard against topography that presents
severe drainage problems. Water-damage lawsuits from the neighbors can be expensive—and you don't want to have to offer potential
buyers a boat! Bear in mind that more asphalt equals more water
run-off; and slopes may translate into fewer lots, thus less profit.
On the other hand, some builders utilize the slope by building the
home into the hillside. This reduces construction costs over those
of a sprawling rambler and cuts fuel expense for buyers. Along the
same lines, try a southern exposure to take advantage of passive
solar heating. Naturally, you'll let buyers know how hard you worked
to reduce their fuel bill and, of course, you'll speak about your
energy-efficient home plans at the hearing.
This thumbnail sketch puts you in the driver's seat regarding
the land itself—but you can't relax yet.

UTILITIES

All along, imagine you're scouting out the terrain for mine-
fields so they won't go off in your face at the hearing. Now consider

utilities: You must detonate this minefield or it will cripple you at the hearing.

If utilities are inadequate, will water and sewer districts agree to lines, pump stations, or whatever is necessary? Find out the capacity of lines and pump stations; make sure water capacity and pressure are adequate or will be made adequate.

One factor in your favor is that some districts are fiefdoms, eager to grow. Here the game is growth. Gamesmanship reached a climax in one case where the proposed building site was midway between two districts. Both districts vied for the utility business. Rivalry erupted. One district promised sewer service—at a discount. It formed a utility local improvement district (ULID), charging property owners $.02 per square foot. Bonds issued by the district paid the bulk of the $400,000 ULID expense, and rate payers throughout the district picked up the bond tab. Outcome of this rivalry still isn't known.

How can you get districts to court you? Examine the sewer and water district comprehensive plan, if any, to see what the plan indicates for the subject and surrounding property. If your property serves as a foot in the door for districts to service a larger area, they may come courting. That's what happened in the $400,000 rivalry case.

Less fortunate developers need to analyze whether the hook-up bill and any ULID assessment will overburden their front-end costs. Do you want to outsmart those costs? Try less front footage, since the bills for sewer lines and street construction hinge on the front footage of the lots in a subdivision. Frontage of 60 feet translates into 60 feet of street expense; 50 feet is cheaper. Using an assessor's map, draw your subdivision to yield the most lots and the least front footage.

Paring costs is also important in regard to protesters: If your profit margin is too thin, you lose flexibility in negotiating with residents (who may bow to your development if you spend a certain amount for landscaping).

Doing this penny-pinching exercise is only half the battle; the unwary face fatal gunfire at the hearing. A stock objection is that development overloads facilities, so build your arsenal to combat that argument. (Even though you work on this defense after property purchase and prior to the hearing, it is presented here to steer you away from an unwise purchase.)

Investigate which public facilities are available or proposed for the area. If you find that the government plans to improve the roadway, to add a park, or to modify the sewer-treatment facility, you can paint a better picture for hearing officials.

To unearth favorable data, read EIS reports from other local projects. Cite findings in your favor to sway decision makers. One area-zoning EIS, for instance, stated that multi-unit demand outstripped supply. This EIS also found that the county park supply would fulfill demand until the year 2000. (Can't you hear yourself now? "Demand outstrips supply, so my condos are necessary to help fulfill demand," you testify, citing the EIS. "And it won't be necessary to add parks since there are already enough to satisfy demand until the year 2000, according to the EIS.") Finally, look for favorable data in city and county growth-management studies, as well as in housing and vacant land studies and from real-estate research organizations.

ZONING: DOES IT BITE?

Developers like John Miller, who sow the seeds of success long before the hearing, concentrate on zoning. What zoning does the city or county comprehensive land-use plan require for your property and for neighboring properties? What does the community land-use plan, if any, call for? The tricky thing is to ferret out which plan prevails: does the county plan prevail over the community plan or vice versa? Prior decisions may provide clues.

If the one that prevails is contrary to what you want, you may want to discredit it. One way that's done is by finding a state law that local government disregarded in the planning process. In Washington State, developers and citizens argue that local government disregarded R.C.W. 36.70 (authority for planning bodies).

Zoning won't bite as much if you choose zoning that accommodates your wishes and the neighbors' wishes. Here's where you can pursue free planning-department assistance. Ask if you can select from high-, medium-, and low-density categories, within multi-unit, commercial, or residential zoning. Generally, the higher the density, the louder the neighbors' screams. You may decide to dampen protest with a lower-density zoning or one calling for less building height. Don't keep your sacrifice a secret from the neighbors.

Another strategy is to apply for the zoning in the comprehensive plan or in the community plan (assuming the zoning is not imposed on the property). Then planners and officials, endowed with pride of authorship, will be more likely to bless your rezone. Riding this route also removes a thorn in your side: you've silenced neighbors who complain that your zoning is inconsistent with the plan. Still another strategy is to apply for high density, figuring you'll get medium density as a compromise.

In some rezones, applicants must prove that circumstances have "substantially changed." "This neighborhood has substantially changed from 15 years earlier," one applicant argued, presenting data. "No, the correct time frame is 5 years earlier, because that's the date of the adoption of the land plan," retorted the challenger. "In the past 5 years, the neighborhood hasn't changed." The lower court judge agreed with the 15-year time frame; the appeal judge disagreed with it. Nevertheless, game players can borrow the ingenuity shown by the applicant in this case.

No single strategy is sure-fire—nor is zoning itself cut-and-dried. A comprehensive-plan map may say one thing; a comprehensive-plan text, another. A community-plan map may say something else. That's why one lawyer advised scrutiny of the following, in light of your proposed use: comprehensive-plan map and text; community-plan map and text; zoning code map and text; shoreline master-program map and text; text of other applicable ordinances, such as moratoria and interim development regulations; text of the capital-improvement program for the area; text of procedural ordinances; text of enabling legislation and important cases; and the latest draft of emerging land-use restrictions for the area. Your jurisdiction may not have all the items listed.

You may discover a bonus in emerging regulations. Ask whether your county or city allows:

Townhouse zoning—it may yield more units per acre, thus more profit.

Single-family zoning with smaller lot sizes—it may also yield more units per acre.

Planned-unit developments—PUDs give more units per acre, in return for clustering homes to provide more green space. On occasion, developers find PUDs more hassle than they're worth.

Potential zoning—it is a second zoning attached to the property, and it recognizes the future suitability of the site for that use. Potential zoning has proven to be a welcome mat for rezones. It does not guarantee a rezone, however.

This peek into the nooks and crannies of zoning doesn't mean that zoning and detailed investigation precede property purchase. Instead, it helps you make a deal with your eyes open.

BUYER BEWARE

Higher-density zoning fuels a higher purchase price. Density means units per acre. Therefore, resolve this question: will the

sales price, on a contingency deal, be based on present zoning or
on the higher value of the property, assuming rezoning or subdividing succeeds ?

On that contingency deal, don't overlook inserting a clause in
the earnest money saying that the seller agrees to join with the purchaser in any proceedings and in the execution of any petition, plats,
or dedications that may be necessary for development (but all without expense to the seller). Beyond that, maybe you should insert a
clause giving you permission to enter the property to make water,
soil, and other tests during the contingency period. An owner may
wish to be indemnified against any liens, should the purchaser arrange for surveys and tests and fail to pay for them. The indemnity
clause is intended to prevent fees from attaching to the land, thus to
the seller.

On the other hand, you don't want to get stuck with the seller's
bills. If the land contains a stand of trees, find out if the land is
under the Forest Tax Law or Open Space Act. If so, specify in the
earnest money whether the buyer or the seller is liable for com-
pensatory property taxes when the property is converted to other
uses. The same thing holds true for farmland. Furthermore, check
on whether you're liable for liens, local improvement district assessments, excise taxes, and so on. What you're doing is protecting your backside.

Actually, most earnest money clauses strive for protection.
For self-protection, include a feasibility clause (also known as an
escape clause) to give yourself a year and a half to see if the necessary permits and zoning can be acquired—or, if you prefer, a "subject to engineering" and "subject to economic feasibility" clause.

By all means do insert a "subject to perc" clause, meaning
the seller has to prove that the soil is deep and porous enough to
accommodate a drain field for a septic tank. Even so, it's wise to
be wary. (Randy Cornelius discovered that the hard way. A licensed
installer of sewer systems pronounced the property Cornelius bought
percable, satisfying his "subject to perc" clause. County officials,
however, told him his perc test was no good because it hadn't been
overseen by a county official. Outcome of the Cornelius case isn't
known yet.) If your land doesn't perc, you can bet that some protester will take potshots at your case in the hearing.

Perc issues and property descriptions—and how to avoid pitfalls—are the meat and potatoes of development. Learn about the
meat and potatoes before eyeing the fine points of the property game,
detailed below. Don't just put the legal property description on the
earnest money. Raw land purchasers may want to include more
than that. Some buyers include a condensed picture of the plat, with
the subject property colored in. Buyers also include a snapshot of

the land and of the section marker and surroundings. Sellers have been known to entice shoppers by moving the section marker to a better piece of neighboring land. The seller is playing bait and switch.

At times, sellers intentionally or inadvertently mislead buyers about the site's size. For self-protection, calculate whether a total price is more realistic than a price-per-acre deal. A survey determines the total purchase price, per acre, in the second method. If the second one is better, insert a clause to that effect in the instrument. Maybe the seller will bear the survey cost.

Further, if the seller holds a lot of land, it may be wise to get an option to buy a given number of acres more at a set price within so many years, then a certain number of acres more, with an acceleration clause should acceleration be desired. Some sellers will want a time limitation, thus preventing the purchaser from tying up their land for an unreasonable amount of time.

Why all this attention to land selection? Latching on to a prime piece of land is crucial because, as the good land disappears, you're left with difficult-to-develop land. Difficult-to-develop land provokes protesters—it commonly has a location or characteristics that spell adverse impact on the neighborhood.

In your search for easy-to-develop land, you may find the ideal site—only the elderly owner won't sell. Don't buck the problem; offer a life-estate deal, under which the property (or the homesite section) reverts to the purchaser upon the death of the owner. This assumes development can proceed, sans the homesite. Simultaneously, search out tax incentives for the seller, then don't hesitate to point them out to Grandma and her heirs. Perhaps you'll work up an exchange, giving Grandma a condo for her 20 acres, in hopes of creating a tax advantage.

Above all, get it in writing. One Kent buyer failed to write in the earnest money that his rental-home price included the appliances. "Those turkeys! I discovered my verbal agreement failed to hold water when the sellers 'took' my appliances," he bristled. Shopping for replacements wasn't fun or cheap.

SAVING $3,000

Your constant companion should be a small voice saying, "Keep your profit picture bright, or you'll be denied flexibility in dealing with protesters." Prevent overpayment, using this easy remedy. That Kent man overpaid $3,000 for his "fixer-upper" because he failed to examine excise-tax records at the courthouse. A member of the Boeing management team, he suffered from inexperience in real estate. He could have offered at least $3,000 less because the buyers had just purchased the rental home a few months earlier for $25,000. They turned a $10,000 profit when he paid them $35,000.

Don't make the same mistake. Examine excise-tax records at the county courthouse to ferret out the last sale price. A $50 tax, in Washington State, translates into a $50,000 price.

In the style of Sherlock Holmes, sleuth out more records. Look up title companies in the Yellow Pages. Then obtain a title report to verify ownership and to pinpoint restrictive covenants, if any. Real-estate agents also get free "take-offs" from the title company. Take-offs detail sales history. Isn't it better to discover a restrictive covenant now, instead of from the mouth of the protester at the hearing? Why not realize a better deal—rather than repeat the Kent man's mistake—by researching records?

Money matters. Scrimp on front-end money so you don't over-price homes. Examples include earnest money payment, sewer and utility costs, permit fees, interest, and return on your own capital. An axiom that follows is that developers who spend less front-end money may underprice you out of business.

LOSING $5 MILLION

Dow Chemical spent a lot of front-end money. "Remember the Dow Chemical case in California? They gave up on a site east of San Francisco Bay after sinking $5 million into obtaining the required permits," recalled Glenn R. Pascall, state Department of Revenue director, then chief of the State Research Council. "They had obtained about 80 permits and had 4 to go when they gave up. The political fall-out was so great that the governor and the legislature had to scramble. But the 'solution' guaranteed no more than a state decision within 18 months—not too swift."

Dow officials probably didn't feel it was too swift to blow $5 million. You may not blow $5 million, but the Dow case sharply illustrates the risks that developers incur, even though most developers work on a smaller scale. Gamblers who don't want to sink a lot of money into a project should search out safeguards. You may ask whether the planning department will tell you about these safeguards. The answer is no: bureaucracies are too big and too busy to mother you. Ask a staffer whether your jurisdiction employs any of these safeguards:

Preapplication conferences let you confer with the staff on your project, giving you a feeling of whether it will fly or flounder.

Preliminary permits let you submit a simple application, minus expensive architectural work. The government staff tells you
whether the basics are right or wrong. If you pass the prelimi-
nary-permit test, you take the second step by applying for a full
permit. In some locations, your preliminary fee offsets the regular application fee.

Contract zoning lets you strike a deal with the council or commission,
in the sense that you both deal in specifics. The council, for example, may say it is interested only in a two-story office building
with 20-foot setbacks. A contract-zone agreement doesn't guarantee that the council will grant the rezone, but your architect
can draw up plans for the council's review without wasting time
or money with plans for a three-story building.

TIMING TIPS

Want a tip-off on how else to save a bundle of money? In a
word: timing. Attempt to second guess what the market will be like
one or two years from now—for it may take two years to get permits,
zoning, and financing. Meanwhile, the old interest meter is running
up your interest charges. To control the interest bill, steer away
from a prolonged battle against protesters.

At the same time, evaluate competition by examining permit
or rezone applications at the planning department. Data are also
available at growth-management departments, although not all jurisdictions have these departments.

If the hearing is two years away, conduct research near the
hearing date so it won't get outdated. Furthermore, you've got to
decide what to build and when to build. The dictum for raw land is
to plan and plat in the wintertime; build in the summertime, avoiding
bad weather. Also, check on when burning permits are issued.

One way to decide what to build is to check real-estate research publications. One publication, Property Dynamics, polled
condo buyers to pinpoint what would appeal to future buyers. Pub-
lisher Timothy Fahey of Kirkland discovered that, next time, buyers
would purchase units with better soundproofing and more closet space.
His poll can cue your future advertising campaign: "Broadmore Es-
tates has better soundproofing and more closet space than other
condos. Come out to the open house today."

PREHEARING PREPARATIONS

You've got to prepare some convincing evidence to present at
the hearing, too. The universal yardstick is that the burden of proof

falls on the applicant. To win, you must prove that your project complies with regulations and fills a need. Can you convince officials that the requested zone conforms with the comprehensive plan; that the application satisfies zone requirements; and that the desired zone is compatible with surrounding land use?

Next, you need to demonstrate a need for the development. Perhaps you can demonstrate a shortage of rental units or housing from data drawn from a real-estate research organization. Can you demonstrate that a major employer or college anticipates expansion, making housing for the influx a need?

Furthermore, how can you prove development won't have adverse impacts on schools, utilities, and roads? Inquire about impact with the school, sewer and water district, and department of public works. If possible, obtain a letter from each regarding impact. Some find that district officials like to point to district capability—like fire-response time—with pride. Boosterism wanes when protesters loom, so don't delay in getting dated letters to submit to the hearing official.

Finally, what proof can you offer on control of water run-off? For starters, state that bales of hay will be used to control run-off.

As you go about your task of rounding up the above information, you'll be contacting the planning department for information. Planners can be very helpful; they can give you ideas on issues ranging from run-off control to landscaping. Developers, however, complain about the hassle of dealing with planning departments; yet, despite the hassle, remind yourself that consideration succeeds better than carping. Above all, don't make the common mistake of telling county employees that your taxes pay for their salaries. Work for cordial relations, because staff members generally pass a recommendation for or against rezoning and so forth on to the next tier of decision makers. Also, don't be afraid to display naïveté.

Normally, developers are always attempting to convince staff members that the proposed use is desirable. However, in the interim stage, the experienced developers restrain advocacy to learn a staffer's true attitude. Staff members react in part according to the press of their workload; frequently, they are extremely busy, scarcely able to devote in-depth study to your project. This works to your advantage if you are considered credible and if you submit factual data that can be the foundation of the planner's report.

The press of workload can also turn into your enemy. When a staffer finds an unclear item or needs additional information, a heavy workload inhibits calls to you. Meanwhile, the application gathers dust. When the lag makes you suspect a snag—call. One developer queries staff members with "Hi, Joe; just checking on whether you need any questions answered in the X file."

Prudent developers also regularly inspect their file. The absence or abundance of protest letters cues their strategy. Developers weigh alternatives, perhaps taking their cue from a lack of letters and "letting sleeping dogs lie." In that sort of situation a developer quietly guides the application through the process. One such applicant won approval of a marina. Other developers head off trouble, preferring not to gamble with meeting the opposition midstream. They contact the neighbors individually, asking either for a letter of support or for supportive hearing testimony.

Strategy to neutralize the opposition also works, sometimes, when the file holds protest letters. Developers meet with the neighbors, both to explain the project and to modify plans to defuse hearing arguments. "I want to hear about any of your concerns" is one way to open the door to dialogue. When the door is open, let residents know about the positive features of the project—attractive architecture, areas to be dedicated to open space, and new shopping or employment opportunities. "Take care to not appear evasive, yet to not reveal information beyond what's asked," warned one old hand.

Developers are cautioned that they may be up against a single-minded homeowners' association. Many times, a past development battle has given birth to a neighborhood group. Leaders are hardcore, no-growth veterans; so it might be easier to side-step contact and deal with neighbors on a one-to-one basis.

Defusing opposition is valuable because decision makers are political animals. Losing your single vote doesn't bother them; losing a neighborhood bloc of support at an election can mean political suicide. Never get trapped into a pre-election hearing date. Find a nonpolitical reason to postpone the hearing until after the election.

The way to turn political instincts to your advantage is to enlist allies. Elicit support from chambers and other local organizations. Encourage them to send supportive letters for the government file on the project. Even lenders can be allies. It's helpful to get a letter from a lender saying that the lender is unwilling to finance construction under current zoning.

"TIGHT MONEY": THE WORDS OF A LENDER
WHO ISN'T KEEN ON MAKING THE LOAN

The lending game itself is worthy of detailed discussion. For newcomers, here's a brief look at how the game is played. Lenders include savings and loan institutions, mortgage firms, the Federal Housing Administration (FHA), and the Veterans Administration (VA).

Some banks are less interested in development loans than in home loans. You should shop among various lenders for the best deal. To evaluate the best deal, consider the amounts of all fees, which may include the loan fee, the release fee, and the prepayment penalty.

Simultaneously, lenders evaluate you and your property. Generally speaking, loan officers are interested in the location of the property, access, topography, availability of utilities, distance to schools and shopping, what kind of reclassification or permit is sought, and more. Lenders want to see an environmental declaration of nonsignificance. They also size up whether you have a good business head. Prepare your financial statement for submission, and apprise the lender that you can cut the deal with a given percentage of profit. If the profit margin is too thin, a lender's interest will be slim; the hesitation stems from the risks that must be taken with the market, as well as with you.

Despite the unpredictability, a lender may see you as the means to get home construction loans and mortgages with Mr. and Mrs. Homebuyer. Aren't these cues for a stronger presentation by you? Do you want to precommit financing for homebuyers?

Document all parts of your presentation package, which should include your:

1. Summary page
2. Description page (see sample)
3. Vicinity map
4. Financial analysis
5. Market analysis
6. Track record, financial statement, and references. (Have you cultivated an acquaintanceship with a lending institution official? If so, she or he should be listed as a reference, along with your lawyer, past builders, real-estate agents, and accountant.)
7. Negative declaration of environmental significance

Some developers borrow enough to "subsidize" the future builder. In this move, builders are loaned part of the price to conserve their capital layout. Actually, the builder then pays interest to the lender, via yourself, so you aren't out anything—but you've sweetened the deal with the builder.

GROUNDWORK

Part of the groundwork for the hearing is maintaining your humor, despite the hassle. For a break, try the game of Build-

SAMPLE DESCRIPTION PAGE

The attached vicinity maps show the location of _____ . It is in the southwest section of King County. It is located on _____, between _____ and _____, about four minutes from the _____ intersection of Interstate 405. The site contains _____ acres and is planned for _____ lots of a minimum size of 7,200 square feet. The density is _____ lots per acre.

Topography is gently to moderately sloping, helping natural drainage and sewage flow. The property is zoned _____ by King County. Public utilities are available at property lines. Interior streets and sidewalks will be required and are included in the financial analysis.

Utilities, proper zoning, and compatibility with surrounding land use make this land particularly good for residential development. The topography and view lot potential should be attractive to buyers. Layout takes advantage of natural amenities.

_____ & Associates was selected as the engineering firm because of their reputation, good rapport with planners, and past performance. The speed with which they obtained preliminary approval of this project speaks well of their abilities.

Several major builders were contacted and received detailed plans. After a complete evaluation by the developers and engineering firm, _____ was selected and a construction contract was negotiated. Construction will be bonded and insured.

The preliminary plat has been approved by the county and all appeal periods have lapsed.

opoly.* Here are some highlights that poke fun at development frustration.

Start: Uncle dies, leaving you 300 buildable acres.
—Go directly to the planning department.

        Swampland requires purchase of 200,000,000 cubic yards of fill.
—Move ahead four spaces.

        Mudslides dump landfill into ocean.
—Lose one turn.

        Interest rates rise.
—Pay $40,000 for buy-down to lower percent.

        High-school civics student files for nuisance injunction.
—Go back to court.

        $5,000 check to councilman bounces.
—Lose one turn.

        Design errors result in no interior plumbing.
—Pay $100,000 for big ditch; merchandise as "Back to Nature."

        Suffer nervous breakdown.
—Pay $20,000 to shrink and lose one turn.

Games aside, you need to consider the following to lay the groundwork for success:

Modify your presentation, if necessary, after examining decisions on earlier, similar cases.

Use a graphic presentation to show the location of the property and related items. As a psychological ploy, splash a lot of green on the map, indicating open space or landscaping. A map rapidly educates decision makers, who often come into the situation cold. They may not be aware of where the property is. With a map, you won't use up your time in answering questions such as "Is your site near Joe's drug store?" from decision makers. In some cases, a map will show that your proposed business site adjoins multi-units, acting

---

*Reproduced by permission of Walker & Lee Real Estate Inc.

as a natural extension to the apartment buffer. Say so. If it shows
good access to main roadways, voice that convincing argument. If
possible, exhibit photos of deteriorating homes nearby to quell neighborhood cries of harming their "well-maintained, stable neighborhood."

Arm yourself with the knowledge of whether a quorum or
majority vote of the decision-making body is necessary. You reduce
your chances if a quorum of five is present (you need four yes votes
from a seven-member body). If the numbers run against you, ask
for a 30-day extension. Request an extension if there are hostile
citizens in the audience since they don't maintain interest well. A
dwindling number may turn out for a future hearing. Plead an excuse that sounds legitimate, like the need for more research on
water run-off.

Take a tape recorder to the hearing. Recordings of outlandish
comments may be useful at a future appeal hearing. You can discredit the opponents.

Decide what to wear. If appearing before a rural board of con-
servative farmers, dress differently from how you would to appear
before a big-city board. If you suspect that board members find certain clothing offensive, rule it out. Rule out smoking, again not to
offend.

Arrange for any witnesses, such as a land consultant, architect, traffic engineer, engineer for sewer and water, or real-estate
agent. An agent who stands to gain by completing your contingency
deal can be counted on to give an especially persuasive presentation.
Save money by scheduling the testimony of witnesses at the beginning
of your presentation, permitting them to leave after speaking. When
witnesses can't attend, submit their letters. It's also wise to submit letters, even of verbal testimony, before the hearing to afford
decision makers a chance to assimilate the contents (assuming they
peruse the file before the hearing). Don't overlook the psychological
point that people don't want to display their ignorance; witnesses giving highly technical testimony are likely to be accepted at face value.

Map out your presentation. Never dwell on troublesome areas.
Address points of conflict, like traffic, at the beginning, because
board attention will be clearest then. Save positive aspects for the
end of the presentation or repeat them then, stamping them into the
minds of board members. One positive argument is a description of
public benefits. For example: "My project will help ease the housing shortage; will help curb energy use through its proximity to employment centers; will help fill under-utilized schools; and will improve a deteriorating, unproductive area. Furthermore, I'm willing
to dedicate land for a park."

Most prehearing preparation centers on anticipating the opponent's argument and marshaling a counterargument. That meeting with the neighbors may have revealed clues to what the opponent's line of attack will be, or letters in the file may tip you off.
Standard homeowner arguments include the following.

Argument: "Traffic congestion will clog our roads and interfere with the safety of our children, especially when they go to
school."
Rebuttal: Counter the argument with figures showing little
difference between traffic generated from your project and the traffic from a project under existing zoning. Ask the department of
public works for appropriate data. Determine whether per hour
formulas from the county or city, from a traffic association, or
from another EIS give the lowest peak traffic count. Use the most
advantageous data. Further, seek out future road improvement
plans from the city, county, and state and submit them.

Argument: "The application is inconsistent with the land-use
plan."
Rebuttal: Plans typically contain a map and a narrative. Hope
that one will be consistent with your project. The narrative, for
example, may say that a policy is to focus growth in an already developed population center or along arterial roads. Point out proximity to the arterial road or center, citing the policy by page number.
If you can't find a leg to stand on, cast a cloud over the plan, saying it's ten years old and outdated.

Argument: "The property should be used under existing
zoning."
Rebuttal: Shop around until you find a lender who will refuse
a loan for existing use. Then submit a letter from the lending institution, refusing to loan money for existing-use development.

THE HEARING: THE GUILLOTINE?

The planning department customarily issues a recommendation for or against the land change, shortly before the hearing. A
call to the department will pinpoint which day you can obtain that report. Reading it ahead of time gives time to counter any negative
points. Be forewarned that opponents may be doing the same thing.
You may want to arrive early to listen to hearing cases scheduled ahead of yours. A preview is of value, if for no other reason
than to quiet anxiety.

Finally, it's your turn. Keep cool and courteous, no matter what. Remind yourself that you've minimized problems by checking the file before the hearing, by bringing chalk or tacks for graphic presentations. The format typically entails a presentation by the developer, one by the opposition, and then an opportunity for rebuttal. Questions from the board may be brief.

After your clear, concise presentation, be prepared to take careful notes on the opponent's testimony. Also be prepared with questions, including the following:

"When and how was your homeowner association formed?"
"How many members do you represent, and how can you demonstrate that number?"
"What alternative would you like to see on my site?"

Don't fall prey to appearing evasive to board questions. If you don't know something, say so, then volunteer to supply the information as soon as possible.

Let the board know you voluntarily sought citizen input. Let them know only a few unresolved points remain, citing specifics.

Convey that you're a good guy. Let the other side be called the bad guys. Then, if you lose, go back to "Go." Do not collect $200.

PART III

Building for the Future

8

THE POLITICS OF
LONG-RANGE REFORM

Reformers are the builders of tomorrow. They are the citizens who shake up tired ways of doing things. They won't tolerate tired government that lets raw sewage flow through their neighborhood creek. They are the developers who strive for a better way, such as Howard Hansen's insistence on proper landscaping. The builders of tomorrow are the ones who resolve disputes between developers and residents, instead of standing by, watching disputes drain monetary and emotional resources—and they are the people at the helm of government with guts enough to stir change. Noble knights? No, you won't see reformers riding white horses in this chapter.

Instead, you'll witness their struggles. It isn't easy for these builders of tomorrow. Entrenched power and procedures resist change. As Charles Hodde puts it later in this chapter, sewer and water districts are "little empires" that resist change; but this state official shakes up their tired way of doing things when he calls for consolidation. Teacher Patti Burgess challenged the status quo when she denounced officials for ducking responsibility for unpopular land plans. In doing so, however, she jeopardized her reappointment to a citizen board. Working for change takes its toll. "I'm burned out," many say. "I'm disheartened," says a boundary board member mentioned later in this chapter.

BOTH SIDES WANT TO SHAPE
LAND USE OF TOMORROW

One band of citizens who wanted to change the status quo squared off against developers who didn't want them to change the status quo. According to Jarlath Hume, it all started out when two ad hoc citizen bands were working for common goals and decided to merge. Hume chaired the first meetings of the County Group in 1978. Stalwarts were veterans of CHECC (Choose an Effective Council), a citizen activist group that helped overturn the old order in Seattle. Founders were from the clean-government troupe that won the State Campaign Disclosure Commission. One member, Seattle University professor Len Mendelbaum, saw a need for change. In his words, Seattle has a high degree of citizen participation and the council works out in the open, but you have little of either at the county council level. The citizen band decided to rate county council candidates. Candidates would be evaluated on the County Group's criteria, pledged Virginia Gunby, a former county freeholder who chaired the Issues Committee.

At the first public meeting, a crowd of 100 discussed criteria and goals—including farmland preservation and concentrating growth in developed areas to relieve the tax burden. At the second public meeting, developers turned out in force to pack the meeting. Parliamentary warfare broke out. The meeting abruptly adjourned with little accomplished. Developer interests had scored a victory. What of the original County Group? Those leaders planned to regather, but the group's fate was uncertain.

Both the developers' leaders and the original leaders of the group knew that working long range—by changing the composition of the council through elections—is more effective than fighting a skirmish over each individual rezone. Neither side wanted to burn up energy, trying to put out the brush fires of individual rezone battles. A leader in another organization also espoused the goal of working long range, instead of putting out brush fires. "People are constantly reacting to zone changes, sewers, and supermarkets," said Edmund Sheridan, assistant director of the Office of Community and Organization Development at the University of Washington. "Many times we've helped by telling them to step back, to stop putting out brush fires."

To work long range, advised Sheridan, find out when government will revamp comprehensive land plans; find out when government is getting ready to apply for or divide up funding. Pressuring of local government works best when it coincides with the planning cycle of government, he stressed. Sheridan recalled how Bellevue residents working with his organization gained about $3 million, including a bond issue for a recreation plan. Community meetings and doorbelling paid off with new sidewalks, a golf course, and a community center, said a pleased Sheridan. The outcome was more successful than most. You don't always get those tangible benefits, he admitted.

MIDGETS WITH MUSCLE MAKE LOCAL HISTORY

The Duwamish Peninsula Community Commission captured
some tangible benefits. "Midgets with muscle" best describes this
citizen-advocate group. Working with a $7,840 annual budget, the
commission exercises clout exceeding its size. Seattle City Councilwoman Jeanette Williams praised the group for tapping $6 million
in government funding when she spoke at a community convention.
The commission sponsored the convention to advance its goal of
building vigorous communities. To further that goal, it uses legal
aid and VISTA workers from the Northwest Institute for Community
Development. It also relies on advice from Tom Gaudette of Chicago,
founder of the Mid-American Institute for Community Development
in Chicago. Saul Alinsky, a Chicago community organizer who left
a tradition of confrontation politics, trained Gaudette. Gaudette believes in the adage, "To the loudest go the spoils."

Being vocal paid off with a $200,000 grant. Trish Gaine,
board chairwoman, explained how the commission won a $200,000
study on Longfellow Creek pollution. The creek carries raw sewage,
as well as creek water, as it winds through the neighborhood. Some
1.2 million gallons of raw sewage flow into the creek annually because pipes for storm water and sewer run-off were never separated,
Gaine declared. She called it a health hazard. So the commission
presented bottled "Longfellow Creek Cider" and "Longfellow Creek-
sickles" to the council, which approved the $200,000 study. The
commission stages things to get the attention of the press, Gaine
explained, citing the "presents" as an example.

The commission's tactics don't draw universal acclaim; but
there's more than one way to shake up tired ways of doing things.
Quietly, Eric Carson worked to change ineffective EIS practices and
to head off showdowns between developers and residents. Carson, a
planner turned consultant, goes between opposing parties, seeking a
common ground. Working on a $36,000 federal mediation grant, he
specializes in mediation (as does the Institute of Environmental
Mediation at the University of Washington). Carson believes there
is an alternative to land-use disputes that sap resources, leaving
losers on all sides. He described how he voluntarily mediated in a
successful case, before he got the grant.

It all started at a county hearing on a request for rezoning 8.5
acres from single-family to multi-units. In the audience were 70
protesters, ready to fight. "Zoning Examiner Joe Lightfoot turned
to me and said, 'Will you mediate?'" Carson recalled; so he embarked on six sessions. He found community resistance toward adding more students to a stuffed school—only the community, caught up

in its fears, had overlooked one factor. Carson reminded residents that condos usually contain working couples, not families with children. That eased some fears.

Carson also addressed the developer's dilemma: he needed to build a set number of units to make a profit. The developer sought 120 units, ultimately settling for 40. Lower density became affordable when $15,000 was added to unit prices, said Carson, who convinced the developer he had underpriced the condos. Carson's research disclosed that the property was in a superior location and that hourly bus lines were coming in, both news to the developer.

Then an incident involving a water fountain made waves. Residents bucked design plans calling for conversion of a low drainage spot into a water fountain. They emphatically did not want an "attractive nuisance" to tempt youngsters. They did not know, however, that there is an alternative to the customary demands for an EIS. The community demanded an EIS, Carson said, but they didn't need an EIS; they just wanted to stop "that poor guy." He persuaded both camps to compromise with $200 of data, instead of a $5,000-$10,000 EIS that would only gather dust. Furthermore, he enlisted help from residents worried about water-fountain hazards. They envisioned youngsters drowning in a deep water fountain. Asked Carson," How can you decorate it to discourage kids ?" Encircle it with prickly trees, they responded, and make the water shallow. Disgruntled people were turning into decision makers. Finally a written pact between the two camps was achieved.

EIS REFORM

Akin to Carson's compromise EIS is collective work that is blazing new EIS frontiers. A city official, for one, issued a limited EIS, dealing only with the housing and transportation effects of proposed apartments. It's a fluid frontier; some officials want one thing, others experiment with something else. In another variation, a single EIS was required for two projects within the same block. This document measured accumulative impact from the two apartment plans. Still another official asked to broaden the scope of an EIS. A hearing examiner, in this case, wouldn't let housing demolishment occur until an EIS was compiled on what impact demolishment would have on the city's tight low-income housing supply. It marked the first time, several observers say, that a local developer had to do an EIS focusing primarily on the social costs of demolishing housing.

By contrast, a traditional EIS format (or none at all) prevails in many counties. Many counties step more slowly into changes in

the EIS and other areas than do cities. Some say longtime county
employees from earlier eras are accustomed to tradition.

HE STEPS SLOWLY INTO CHANGE

Ed Sand is one such veteran. During almost three decades in
county planning, he has held more hearings and reviewed more Environmental Impact Statements than he can recall. Deliberate and
practical-minded, Sand directs the county Building and Land Development Division (BALD). When asked about one method of better
controlling water run-off, Sand weighed whether it could be enacted.
"I don't know if we can sell it, politically," he said. He was
more optimistic about establishing a requirement for a site-plan permit. A permit would precede land clearing. There had been some
thought about a site-plan permit, Sand said, adding that it would be
proposed. Then he weighed consequences of another change afoot.
There had been talk of posting notice of short plats (a parcel about
to be divided into four lots or fewer). Any situation in which government gives notice generally costs tax money. Sand said that expanding notice to short plats would be a fantastically costly mistake, and
that the measure would just lead people astray, since nothing could
be done anyway. BALD doesn't hold hearings on short plats.
Other changes then under council consideration included re-
leasing prehearing reports 14 days prior to the hearing, instead of
the customary 7 days. Sand did not welcome the new 14-day time
frame. He preferred the old time frame, since "7 days is adequate."
Even so, he said, the county is ahead of some other jurisdictions,
which don't issue any prehearing report. That's just one area, Sand
said, in which county land practices are superior to those of other
governments.
Leaning back in his chair, Sand mused about the attitude of the
public toward BALD. He finds contradictory perceptions of his division, staffed by about 100. Some perceive a progrowth division,
while others perceive a no-growth division. Some people think we're
no-growth; they see zonings, EISs, and community plans, he said,
adding that others perceive a progrowth attitude in the expediting of
permits. In Sand's words, half the office is in a hurry, half is putting on the brakes—it gets to be a funny situation.

"A PLANNER IS A POLITICIAN IN DISGUISE"

Like Sand, Fred Stouder is a veteran planning director. Unlike Sand, Stouder left the public sector. Stouder turned his back on

20 years as a civil servant—but not on his ideals. This former
Yakima planning director calls himself a community advocate. Still
a Peace Corpsman in thought, this state-wide land-use consultant
faulted bureaucrats. He issued a stern warning about excessive
power enjoyed by planners, some of whom play politician instead of
public servant.

"A planner is a politician in disguise," Stouder declared. "For
years, I was a public servant, and we were 'protecting the public
good.' It can be dangerous. We see excesses at all levels. We
planners succumb." Stouder continued to illustrate how planners
tilt the balance. "As a planner, I didn't have enough sympathy for
the cash-flow problems of the developer. Long waits, rezones, eat
up time. Time costs money. After months of waiting, the little guy
is broke. The big ones will win: they can wait you out." He regrets
that delay drives "the little guy" out. His clients include cities and
the state Association of Cities.

REFORMERS CAN LEARN FROM THESE LESSONS

There weren't any Fred Stouders around to blow the whistle
when a crowd of 900 protested massive county rezones. No one in
the crowd knew that the county's method of receiving input suffered
from a gap. No one announced that testimony should also be submitted in writing in order to be considered. While there was silence
on that score, there was plenty of noise in the hearing auditorium.
Controversy came to a boil when the crowd of 900 protested the Highline "area-zoning" plan. They didn't accept the county explanation
that area rezones would make existing zoning conform with the 1977
community plan. Most were angry at becoming what they called "a
dumping ground" for growth. Maintaining single-family zoning
brought favorable testimony from 26 speakers; they testified against
area-zoning plans to rezone land to higher density (units per acre)
to accommodate growth. "Our taxes will go up because our land will
increase in value," objected Cynthia Carper, presenting petitions
from 152 neighbors. When the battle subsided at the end of the hearing, the score was 26 to 6, in favor of lower, single-family zoning.
Only 6 speakers testified in favor of higher density. The battle was
refought in a series of hearings that followed. County officials at
each hearing repeated the county litany—the responsibility for area
zoning rests with the 1977 community-plan citizen committee.

One committee member blew the whistle. "Quit making us the
scapegoats! Stop passing the buck!" bristled teacher Patti Burgess
at a subsequent hearing. Fellow committee members echoed her,
saying that county officials and planners devised the 1977 plan after

naïve committee members voiced support for such concepts as pre-
serving single-family neighborhoods. Committee members felt be-
trayed by the county. Crowds of developers and homeowners thought
the county council was passing the buck when Councilman Paul Barden
repeatedly said that the county executive branch—not his legislative
(council) branch—drew up area zoning based "on the community's
wishes." "Never have I been to a meeting as confrontive as this one,"
said a surprised Barden, a veteran of 13 years in politics. Another
councilman said he was lucky he didn't get lynched.

Despite this series of hearings, the following procedural gaps
may have rendered some citizens voiceless. First, no announce-
ment was made to the assembly of 900 that only written testimony
regarding objections to zoning changes would be considered. Verbal
testimony may have been in vain. The lesson for other citizens and
developers? Don't be disfranchised; always put it in writing. Second,
the county issued an EIS on area zoning after—not before—the community hearings, causing local lawyer Llewellyn Matthews to charge
that the county undermined the citizen-participation process. The
EIS report told how area zoning would change the character of the
community and measured other impacts, thus helping the reader
evaluate area zoning. Third, two zoning changes were at hand simultaneously. The area-zoning plan already covered 1,956 acres. In
addition, some 400 Highline owners accepted the county's invitation
to request a rezone for land not in the plan; but the county failed to
adhere to rezone notification requirements. Then angry owners,
such as Ginger Babcock, threatened litigation because they weren't
notified of owner-initiated applications. Under conventional rezones,
abutting owners like Babcock receive mailed notice of a hearing.
Babcock inadvertently found out about a $1.7 million multi-unit ap-
plication, she said. By chance, other owners learned about an application for a rezone for a $10 million project. What did the county
say about gaps?

The county was overwhelmed, Jack Lynch said, in response to
criticism of procedural gaps. Director of the county Department of
Planning and Community Development, he pointed a finger of blame
at the council. "They set up the meetings," he said. Perhaps,
Lynch went on, a listing of the 400 applications could be made available before the final council hearing that would make area-zoning
decisions. However, Lynch added, that would be up to the council.

Other officials admitted the county made mistakes at the onset.
County missteps surfaced with Highline because it was "the guinea
pig," to use County Councilman R. R. "Bob" Greive's words. The
key question at the onset is whether a county should update the overall comprehensive land plan first or create community plans first.
In retrospect, County Councilman Bruce Laing regretted that the

1964 comprehensive plan wasn't updated first, before most of the
13 community plans. That would have been ideal, he explained.
County rationale for community plans was first to build a constituency for growth management, recalled Keith Dearborn, then a county
planning official. To build a constituency, the county appointed
Burgess and others to community-plan committees.

In fact, it build a constituency of disgruntled property owners,
rejoined Bruce Chapman, then secretary of state and gubernatorial
rival of John Spellman. Meanwhile, the county left the comprehensive plan update on the back burner for years; but it was expected to
emerge for full public debate. The update, known as the Development Guide report, called for growth management, using "in-fill"
(developing vacant lots in settled communities to utilize existing
utilities) to accommodate growth.

INSIDER KEEPS CLOSE WATCH
ON GOVERNMENT PANEL

Clearly, other locales can use the county's experience as a
crystal ball. Land use just isn't static—anywhere. Land use isn't
static because growth occurs and because population shifts, so government works on land plans and on boundary changes. One arm of
government is designed to regulate sewer districts and cities that
want to change their boundaries. When growth is foreseen for an
unsewered area, for example, the sewer district may want to enlarge its boundaries. When, to use another example, an area wants
to annex (pull out from the county to unite with an adjoining city) or
to incorporate (form a city), proponents must petition a county boundary review board. Citizen board members hold hearings, then issue
rulings, approving or rejecting annexation or incorporation. Both
represent massive land-use changes that stamp their consequences
on taxes, lifestyle, and government services (or lack of them).

Peter Burgess, one of 12 citizen board members, blew the
whistle on the board. He charged that it didn't discharge all its
duties. The County Boundary Review Board makes critical land-
use decisions—without necessarily reviewing all the facts, Burgess
charged, adding that there have been cases where the board has approved annexation, where rejection was justified. It may appear
that the board is a rubber stamp, Burgess said.

He didn't want inadequate review to hurt people; yet when a
city annexed one area, the residents in the annexed area were left
virtually unprotected against fire, declared Burgess, a former fire
commissioner. Mutual-aid agreements were canceled; a person
could burn to death because of the long response time, he warned.

When a city takes in an annexed area, it should give fire protection and other services commensurate with the tax revenue generated by the area, Burgess declared; yet annexation takes place
with no regard for units of local government or for services for
which people pay taxes.

One tool for better scrutiny is an EIS, Burgess believes. However, few governments step forward with an EIS. The board should
look at an EIS when it reviews an annexation, he said, adding that 99
percent of city annex applications say there's no significant impact.
"Hogwash! Any time you annex a large rural area into a city, you
impact traffic patterns, police, a whole multitude of things," he declared. Moreover, Burgess said, the board should heed community
land-use plans and should require that developers disclose their
plans when annexation to a sewer district is desired. Burgess said
that the question that pushes most annexations is how many units can
be gotten out of an acre. Money controls our growth today, he
lamented.

Burgess admits he's "an independent voice." He argued
against an annexation, this time in Auburn. "I'm disheartened," he
said after the annexation had been approved, adding that approval
established an annexation with irregular boundaries. Under state
law, the board should aim for formation of even boundaries. It was
frustrating to see the board go against state law, the Boeing planner
said. In defense, Brice Martin, the chief staffer, said that only two
mistakes, out of thousands of cases in 12 years, is not a bad score.
Martin said in retrospect that the board made a mistake years ago
when it accepted Bothell's request to annex "a long leg" across the
Sammamish Valley with "a fist on the end of it." The second mistake was formation of the Holiday Lake Sewer District, according to
Martin.

In response to the EIS challenge issued by Burgess, Martin
finds gaps too. Only what Martin finds is this: the board insists on
an environmental assessment from a city, he said, adding that it's
not uncommon to get an inadequate one. The EIS issue boils down to
who is going to pay for the EIS. The board can't pick up the tab,
Martin argued; and he countered Burgess' contention that the board
should reject annexation, where justified. The board is like any
regulatory body, Martin responded, adding that its sheer existence
is enough to deter 90 percent of the problems. Martin takes exception to Burgess' call for earlier staff reports to the board, saying
that a number of agencies don't send reviews back until the last
minute.

"Sometimes we get conflicting evidence. For example, water
district officials will say it has sufficient capacity and reservoirs.
But that doesn't tell me the water pressure and volume at the annex

site," Martin explained. "Then the developer will say, 'Yes, every-thing's available.' But when I talk to the fire chief, he says water is insufficient. So we haul the respective engineers on the carpet. Sometimes we get satisfactory answers. Sometimes we get frus-trated from unsatisfactory answers."

THE LEFT HAND DOESN'T KNOW WHAT
THE RIGHT HAND IS DOING

Water, sewer, and other junior taxing districts evoke a lot of frustration. It's easy to see why, Robert Bradford said. As execu-tive director of the Seattle Professional Engineering Employees Association (SPEEA), which represents more than 14,000 Boeing engineers, he was involved in developing a new $900,000 headquar-ters for the organization. Boundaries of two districts cut across the SPEEA site, but Bradford found the districts failed to co-ordinate with one another. SPEEA people were surprised that each district uses a different size of water pipe; Bradford could hardly believe that there was a two-inch difference in pipe diameter.

Once entrenched, they're all little empires, Charles Hodde said of junior districts. This state official called for reform. There's no excuse for having more than 3,000 tax districts in this state, he said, adding that about 2,000 water, sewer, and other dis-tricts are in King County alone. Hodde urged transferring many district activities to the county council for efficiency. Junior dis-tricts levy taxes, carry out assessments, and bill utility customers, as well as lay pipe and fight fires.

Moreover, the same theme of discontent swirls around several levels of government, from the local up to the national scene. Critics commonly complain that government units fail to co-ordinate with one another. The criticism may be voiced as a complaint against the disparities between HUD and FHA and other financing mechanisms; against the conflicts between HUD and local levels; or against the lack of co-ordination by a city and county that are neighbors. Such complaints reflect a contemporary situation in which the left hand doesn't know what the right hand is doing.

One remedy is better communication between neighboring offi-cials. Another is establishment of a regional council, a mechanism that has been employed by numerous governments across the coun-try. However, some regional councils are paper tigers, unable to punish violators. They lack teeth, and only add another layer of paperwork in the pathway of development. The Metropolitan Council of the Twin Cities Area in Minnesota—apart from any judgment of the council's merits—does have teeth in terms of taxing power.

Funds to support the council come from federal and state governments, from regional commissions, and from a property tax levy
collected in the region, states the Citizen Guide to the Metropolitan
Council. The region encompasses seven counties. Perhaps as a
consequence, the Twin Cities area has developed a relatively strong
regional government structure, said Ted Smebakken of the council.
The council is authorized to:

1. Prepare a long-range regional plan upon which to base development decisions
2. Review applications for federal and state funds to assure consis-
   tency with the regional plan
3. Prepare policy plans to give development direction to public
   transit, regional parks, airports, housing, and water-quality
   management activities
4. Approve financial plans of regional agencies
5. Administer a park-financing program to implement development
   of the regional park system
6. Administer Metropolitan Housing and Redevelopment Authority
   programs
7. Make recommendations to the state on health-care facility needs
8. Make grants in the aging and arts areas

Fortunately, all these builders of tomorrow are beacons that
light the way to better ways of doing things. This chapter has presented only vignettes of reform, however. It is up to fellow developers, citizens, and officials to draw on the ideas or lessons to fit
other situations. Nevertheless, items of lasting value emerge from
these vignettes: don't trust government—put testimony in writing;
don't fight individual rezone brush fires—instead, work long range;
and streamline the zoning process so the "little guy" isn't driven out
of the development business. A final message is this: be thankful
that whistle blowers rock the inertia and entrenched power built into
the system.

9

GOVERNMENT CAN BE
THE GOOD GUY

Do you feel disillusioned when reading news reports? Take heart. In this chapter, you won't read about the campaign rival who accused the incumbent of turning a profit when a newly constructed freeway exit created a shopping center on the raw land the incumbent bought early on; nor will you read about those councilmen who rigged rezones, or certain judges who bend land-use interpretations to curry favor with those who appoint federal judges. (Actually, close observers deduce the judicial story by reading in between the lines; they see the probusiness rulings and they see the congressional nod from one who relies on business campaign contributions.)

Instead, this chapter is devoted to an examination of how certain city leaders engineer procedures that prevent pay-offs, and how some judges have engineered procedures and precedents that protect the public good and private-property rights. In government's system of checks and balances, courts can act as a check against city and county administrative decisions.

INGREDIENTS OF INTEGRITY

As government sails toward the Isle of Integrity, there are several hands on board—builders, citizens, and staff reformers. One government, Arlington Heights, Illinois, reached the Isle of Integrity because several winds were blowing in its favor: disclosure practices, for one thing; cross-checking within the system, for another; integrity at city hall, for yet another; and, finally, citizens and builders who had a stake in a good system. A closer look, now, sheds light on how Arlington Heights charted its course.

To begin with, builders who want to protect their reputation and revenue from sales have an inherent stake in a good system. As John A. Gardiner relates: "One contractor noted simply, 'Why should we pay off to avoid the building codes? . . . We have a steady demand for high quality houses, and buyers would spot shoddy construction. Therefore, builders have a stake in a good inspection system.'"* The mere presence of vocal developers can act as a deterrent, such as when John Q. Government mulls things over: "We'd better not impose a total sewer moratorium or unduly strict standards, or let citizens get their way all the time. Otherwise developers will bug us, back other candidates at the ballot box, and take us to task in court." The same deterrent dynamic can hold true for citizens.

Like builders, citizens have a stake in a good system. The impetus behind citizen activism is that citizens want to preserve their lifestyle and protect their property values. Affluence accentuates protectiveness toward property values. A prestigious community typically seeks to maintain prestige, since prestige is believed to keep property values high. This stifles slapdash construction. For example, affluence in Arlington Heights inhibits corruption and poor construction. It all starts out when Arlington Heights' voters elect citizen servants—village presidents and trustees have frequently been lawyers or corporate executives—who are accustomed to high-quality help. They set salaries that apparently attract high-quality employees, according to Gardiner. The city manager was paid $51,750; department chiefs received between $28,000 and $36,000, according to the city. Developers can't outsmart employees who have technical expertise, so developers have to adhere to standards. Additionally, an expert staff will generally update the zoning code, again instilling high standards.

---

*John A. Gardiner, Theodore R. Lyman, and Steven A. Waldhorn, Corruption in Land Use and Building Regulation, Vol. 2 (Washington, D.C.: National Institute of Law Enforcement and Criminal Justice, 1979), "Appendix: Case Studies of Corruption and Reform." Reprinted by permission. The references in this chapter are to Gardiner's case studies in that work. These materials were analyzed in greater depth in John A. Gardiner and Theodore R. Lyman, Decisions for Sale: Corruption in Zoning and Building Regulation (New York: Praeger, 1978). Gardiner is a political science professor at the University of Illinois, at Chicago Circle. Lyman is deputy director of the Center for Public Policy Research at SRI International, and Waldhorn is a senior policy analyst at SRI International.

DISCLOSURE PRACTICES

Admittedly, less affluent communities will find it hard to follow in Arlington Heights' footsteps every step of the way—but they
can take heart, because disclosure practices are easy to copy. Disclosure practices proved their worth when they helped two jurisdictions steer a steady course, despite corruption close at hand. First,
Gardiner credits disclosure practices for helping Fairfax County,
Virginia. He's convinced that today's integrity is a continuation of
long-standing practices and that the community at large was not involved in past zoning scandals. Old-timers recall how the "squirearchy" used to dominate the county. The squirearchy was the "old-
boy network" of large landowners, according to Gardiner. He states
that in 1966, after a grand jury scrutinized 12 rezonings, the U.S.
Justice Department issued indictments against six developers, five
supervisors (a supervisor is akin to a councilman), two zoning lawyers, the county planning director, and his deputy.

Second, Arlington Heights is, ironically, located in Illinois—
the home of Chicago, Cook County, and machine politics. Indeed,
Arlington Heights is in Chicago's backyard. Surrounded by an environment in which minor pay-offs to building inspectors were common and many local officials grew rich through the sale of zoning
variances, Arlington Heights developed as a model of righteousness,
Gardiner wrote. This model of righteousness exercises strict control over its employees, Gardiner stated, detailing the following
controls.

One form of control is that moonlighting falls under the scrutiny of the supervisor. "Outside work is permitted to the extent that
it does not prevent employees from devoting their primary interest
to the accomplishment of their work for the [Arlington Heights] village or tend to create a conflict between the private interests of the
employee and the employee's official responsibility," stated the city
manager's August 4, 1975, memo to department heads. Specifically,
the memo stated, an employee shall not perform outside work:

1. Which is of such a nature that it may be reasonably construed by
   the public to be the official act of the department
2. Which involves the use of village facilities, equipment, and supplies
3. Which involves the use of official information not available to the
   public
4. Which might encourage on the part of the general public, a reasonable belief of a conflict of interest

While an employee is not prohibited from performing outside work,
solely because the work is of the same general nature as the work

he or she performs for Arlington Heights, no employee may perform
outside work if:

1. The work is such that the employee would be expected to do it
   as part of his or her regular duties
2. The work involved management of a business closely related to
   the official work of the employee
3. The work would tend to influence the exercise of impartial judgment on any matter coming before the employee in the course of
   his or her official duties

CODE OF ETHICS

Elected and appointed officials, as well as employees earning
more than $20,000 per year, must adhere to a code of ethics in
Arlington Heights, according to Gardiner. Violators are subject to
a $500 penalty per offense. Under the code, an individual must dis-
close all outside employment, all real-estate holdings owned within
the village, and all ownership interests in firms doing business with
the village. "No elected or appointed official or employee of the village, whether paid or unpaid, shall engage in any business or transaction or shall have a financial or other interest, direct or indirect,
which is incompatible with the proper discharge of his official duties
in the public interest or would tend to impair his independence of
judgment or action in the performance of his official duties," the
code states.

GIFTS FORBIDDEN

Accepting gifts impairs independence, too. Gardiner found
that the village manager regards gifts and free meals as first-step
compromises upon the "arm's length" posture that officials must
maintain. The village manager lets gift givers know he means business. He has sent this letter to firms doing business with the city.

Gentlemen:
We are again approaching the Holiday Season. We
wish we had a way that we could remember each of our
contractors and suppliers for their helpfulness during
the year. Unfortunately, being a public agency, there
is no way this can be done. We hope you will understand, and, of course, we would be embarrassed if you
thought of us with more than a card.

In order to continue cordial but impartial relations with all firms doing business, and to insure the
public's continued confidence in our Village Government, we appreciate your past cooperation in honor-
ing the village's request that you omit the names of
all elected officials as well as employees of the village from your holiday list.

Sincerely yours,

Village manager

DISCLOSURE

Arlington Heights exercises strict control over its employees,
according to Gardiner. It requires annual disclosure of outside employment and financial interests. Employees—like elected officials
in some states—must report outside positions or businesses in which
they have a financial interest. The village also gives the disclosure
message to applicants for department-head positions, since applicants must detail their financial status.

CRACKING DOWN ON DEVELOPERS

Disclosure extends to the other side of the fence, too. First,
rezone applications must bear the names of all current owners.
This thwarts the disguises commonly employed by developer-
applicants.

Second, each building-permit application must climb a ladder
of reviews. Beginning at the bottom of the ladder, an application is
submitted to the department of building and zoning. There, it is
reviewed by an architectural committee, chaired by a local architect. The committee checks design. Stepping up the ladder, the
application is reviewed by the engineering department for grades
and drainage. Near the top of the ladder, it is reviewed by electrical, structural, plumbing, and zoning inspectors. Inspectors
visit each site at least twice—once for a rough inspection prior to
drywall, next for a final inspection. If everything is O.K., the department director grants the permit. The department director also
makes on-site spot checks.

ENGINEERING INTEGRITY

It is easier to copy inspection and other techniques than it is
to duplicate the human element. The human element touches the

heart of government itself: the village manager of Arlington Heights.
He has engineered integrity, Gardiner observed.

"A final factor, uppermost in the minds of virtually everyone
asked to explain the norm of integrity found throughout the community, is the leadership the current manager has brought to the manager's office," Gardiner stated. "For over 18 years, he has super-
vised the tripling of the city's population, the recruitment and retention of loyal and professional department heads and had a spotless
reputation for integrity."

PIGGYBACK RIDES

Another government insider, Snohomish County Zoning Examiner John Galt, also strives to engineer integrity. Galt knows
that local government must ride herd on developers and protesters,
just as the courts ride herd on the excesses of local government.
Galt sounded the alarm on "piggyback" game players who want to
outsmart government. Developers have mastered the game of piggyback, knowing they can slice subdivision expense. Directions for
piggyback are easy. Game players know they can get one short plat
(four lots or fewer) approved; then get a second, adjacent short plat
approved; and so on until they have piggybacked enough short plats
to achieve the same amount of space that is encompassed by a subdivision (more than four lots). Subdivision applicants typically incur
expense for interior roads, but piggyback riders shave expense because short-plat road requirements are usually less—or nil. Galt,
though, is catching on. In the first six months of 1979, developers
created twice as many short plats as formally platted lots, Galt said,
adding that this trend continues in other years.

Knowing that road construction was shortchanged, Galt sowed
the seeds of reform by calling for a road review. He called for a
comprehensive review of the impact of short platting upon the county's
road needs. There is a real question in Galt's mind about whether
the future road network needs of the county are being met by short
plats. His lesson on piggybacking can be borrowed by other jurisdictions that suffer from excessive short plats. For example, half
of the total number of Thurston County lots—about 3,000—were
created with short plats, according to the regional planning commission director. He warned that there may be proposals to raise short
plat standards there.

Galt's work exemplifies the cross-checking mechanism that
any jurisdiction could copy. To begin with, Galt issues semiannual
reports to prod the county. Persistent, Galt then issues a "report
card" in a subsequent report. Here, he cites county progress—or

lack of it—on his proposed reforms. In his reports, he seeks to ex-
act reforms for the public and for the developer, as illustrated below. In his reforms, Galt wants to:

Begin master applications and preapplication conferences between
    developers and staff
End independent action by the health department (approval of sewer
    and water); the planning department (zoning and setbacks); the
    public-works department (road and driveway permits); and the
    building department (foundation approval). Instead, co-ordinate
    and integrate these things to reduce the margin for error, Galt
    urged, and don't let citizen and developer bewilderment and
    costly mistakes continue.
Streamline. Instead of treating EIS and planning reviews separately,
    he said, explore ways to reduce or eliminate this redundancy.
Modify unnecessarily harsh laws
Rewrite the subdivision code, which he said is in terrible shape
Continue issuance of the examiner's report. It has contained data
    on trends and growth hot spots. It also has tipped off readers
    who wanted to gauge the rezone attitude of decision makers,
    since data indicated how many times the council/commission con-
    curred with the examiner. All in all, observers say, it is must
    reading for developers and citizens.

BETTER NOTIFICATION

In his reports, Galt vividly illustrates his cross-checking technique when he faults those who issue hearing notices. Galt said the
county's method of mailing legal notices suffers from a flaw that has
been well known for many years. The system uses the assessor's
computerized parcel file as the source of the names and addresses
of surrounding landowners. The county informs surrounding owners
about hearings. However, he said, where a resident has a mortgage
with a reserve account for taxes, the lender's address, rather than
the borrower's, is the one in the assessor's files. It is then up to
the lender to forward the hearing notice to the borrower, Galt explained, but lenders have a very spotty record in this area—so
people suffer.
The unfortunate result is that many people get the notice a
short time before or some time after the hearing—or never, he
added, noting that people frequently express strong feelings about
the shortness of notice or lack of notice when they testify.
Galt sees a solution to this problem, which plagues many
jurisdictions. Place responsibility for developing the list of adjacent property owners upon each applicant, he advised. Applicants

should be required to research the assessor's and auditor's records
to develop an accurate list of legal property owners, Galt urged,
adding that certain cities employ this method because they do not
have the staff to compile a list of owners.

Inadequate notice is a sore spot that irritates communities,
whether a mailed notice or a posted notice at the site is the customary procedure. Yet inadequate notice is relatively easy to correct.
For example, Vancouver, British Columbia, began using four-foot
by eight-foot signs in 1975 for developments of major impact, which
formed about 5 percent of reclassifications. The $250 sign cost was
borne by the applicant, who was also responsible for posting. Benefits indicated that the posting of large signs should be continued, according to A. R. Floyd of the Vancouver Zoning Division.

Perhaps unwittingly following in the footsteps of Vancouver,
King County started a pilot program, using large "For Sale"-sized
signs for rezone notification. Government listened when the Shoreline Community Plan Committee in 1978 recommended use of "For
Sale"-type signs. The committee originated when the county appointed a dozen committees, usually balanced between citizens and
developers, to help revamp the comprehensive land-use plan.
(Shoreline's seedbed germinated other ideas for improvement, including one that would prohibit auto access to medium- and high-
density multiple-family complexes through residential neighborhoods.
By implication, high-density units should be located by arterial
roads.) Shoreline's "For Sale"-sign work is an example of how citizen activism exerts a check on government.

Notification goes hand in hand with where and when hearings
are scheduled. Inconvenient hearings provoke complaints from citizens who resent being denied input. Critics believe daytime hearings in a downtown courthouse or city hall bar full and convenient
citizen testimony. In particular, they say, daytime hearings work
a hardship on employees who must take time off from work to testify.

Bruce Laing, then a zoning examiner, didn't turn a deaf ear to
these complaints. Like Galt, he worked to open the door for input.
Laing asked the county council for $223,960 to hold community hear-
ings in the evening. The council approved $11,000 for a pilot project
in mid-1979. Various examiners then conducted daytime and night-
time hearings in rent-free city halls in outlying areas—drawing raves
from hearing participants.

However, reforms that draw raves may die on the drawing
board when the change entails shifting power away from one part of
government. That was the case when Laing, along with a county
planning and community development committee, advanced another
idea. Laing and the committee both advocated shifting decisions on
rezones and reclassifications away from the council to a nonelected

zoning administrator, except for certain cases. Currently, the examiner holds the power of making recommendations; the council holds the power of final decision. The council resisted any change; characteristically, councils are reluctant to relinquish power. (However, some council members didn't hesitate to take the credit for King County's widely copied zoning-examiner system, established in 1969 as one of the first two systems in counties across the nation.)

Laing, an examiner since 1969, continues to tinker with the land-use system, just as a master mechanic tunes up a car. Now he tunes things up as a newly elected county councilman. Not far away, in the courthouse complex, county Building Inspector Supervisor Dave Peterson finds that the land-use engine is misfiring. In his diagnosis, the building boom causes construction on many sites formerly thought too steep. Water run-off then exacts a toll. In one incident, a wall of mud slipped onto miles of a Renton road from the large development of homes up above. Peterson believes that the incident reaffirmed the need for action. He contended that the time to work on the problem is before the water hits the streets and added that he is working to combat the problem.

COURTS HAVE CLOUT

The invisible hand of the court acts as a check, guiding city and county government along. For example, a county prosecutor cited Euclid v. Ambler Realty Co., a 1926 U.S. Supreme Court case where the high court upheld zoning, itself, as a land-use tool. (Note that only a half dozen zoning cases have reached the high court because zoning usually falls in the province of lower courts.) The Cleveland-area realty had argued that zoning of one section restricted marketability of its entire tract. Citing Euclid and other authority, the prosecutor said that the council can downzone (reduce use) and make other zoning decisions, based on valid health, safety, and general welfare reasons, and that a determination to downzone could properly be based on numerous grounds—for example, to control run-off, to accommodate septic tanks, to avoid air and water pollution, or to control overloading of existing public facilities. Individuals who pursue court remedies should ponder whether the action falls within the government's police powers; and whether the action was arbitrary and capricious.

One developer group decided to pursue a court remedy because it felt the city had exceeded its police power. It all started out when Petaluma, California, limited construction to 500 new units per year, to retain its small-town character and to remain within capital-budget constraints. The Construction Industry Association of Sonoma County brought suit, charging that the city had exceeded its police power and that it had violated constitutional civil rights. The federal district court upheld the builders. Then the Ninth Circuit Court of Appeals reversed the decision, reasoning that all zoning to some extent excludes some uses and structures.

A case in Ramapo, New York, centered on the same issue as the Petaluma case: whether and how a city or county can limit growth. Unlike Petaluma, Ramapo laid the groundwork to pass the court test. Every proposal to develop any residential subdivision of two or more lots was subject to approval by the town board. Proposals were evaluated according to a point system based on the readiness of the site for development—that is, on the number of public services available at the site or on the number of services the developer was willing to furnish. More importantly, Ramapo called for phasing in a program of low-income housing. Ramapo was rewarded when the court of appeals sustained its growth-limit plan. Courts generally uphold an attempt to slow growth when the plan doesn't exclude minorities; when the halt is temporary; and when the community wishes to buy time to get a handle on growth, rather than to stop growth. That is the finding of a national League of Women Voters publication, Growth and Land Use: Shaping Future Patterns (League of Women

Voters Education Fund, 1977). Ramapo apparently satisfied the
court's expectations.

The importance of the courts, in both procedure and precedent,
should not be overlooked by land-use players. One landmark case
that demonstrates both aspects originated when the Bothell City Council granted a rezone from an agricultural to a business-commercial
classification. But SAVE (Save A Valuable Environment), a citizen
group, didn't want a shopping center on the 141 acres. The clash
between citizens and city fathers culminated when the state Supreme
Court upheld the citizens in SAVE v. Bothell. Procedurally, the
justices found that some city fathers had violated the Appearance of
Fairness Doctrine, which insists that decision makers appear impartial. The court thus acted as a check against the city. Beyond
that, justices acted as a check when they ruled against the 141-acre
"spot zoning."

More importantly, justices established a precedent on substantive issues when they held that the effect of a proposal on the
entire area must be considered. Now selfish municipalities may not
survive a court test. The significance of SAVE, lawyer Roger Leed
said, is painfully evident in the conversion of the rich farmland in
the Green River Valley into paved parking lots, miles of warehouses,
and shopping centers. Valley urbanization occurred because little
municipalities—in their eagerness to build up their tax bases—didn't
consider regional impacts, he explained. If the 1978 SAVE decision
had been handed down ten years earlier, the Green River Valley
probably wouldn't be urbanized, said Leed, who specializes in land
use and environment.

He singled out SAVE as probably the most important ruling in
state land law. He also called Parkridge v. Seattle significant.
This clash began when the city downzoned a developer's apartment-
house site from multi-unit to single-family, and rejected his application for an apartment-house building permit. In Parkridge, the
state Supreme Court in 1978 upheld the developer's rights to existing zoning. The high court recognized that developers have private-
property rights. In effect, justices were acting as a check on local
government—they, essentially, reversed the city's decision, saying
that it was unfair to the developer. The bench left a stern warning
for wayward local government to ponder.

This ruling places a heavy burden on local governments to show
that significant circumstances have changed or that a mistake was
made, Leed said. Local government just can't expect to "monkey
around" with zoning, he added. According to Leed, this ruling
basically acts to lend stability.

Lawyer Aramburu also believes the high court strengthens orderly land use. His conclusion was drawn from several rulings,

including SAVE, Narrows View Community Association v. Tacoma, and Smith v. Skagit County. In SAVE, the court called spot zoning illegal and it affirmed that Bothell had violated the Appearance of Fairness Doctrine (which says decision makers must appear impartial). The court also found that Tacoma's rezone had violated the doctrine, so the Narrows View Community Association won its appeal. The court upheld the appeal against Skagit County's rezone of one-fifth of Guemes Island, on grounds that the county had violated the Appearance of Fairness Doctrine and on grounds that Skagit County had approved spot zoning for the aluminum plant. The court's message is that orderly land-use decisions will stand up better in court than disorderly decisions will. A further illustration of the direction the courts are moving is that some courts are making council hearings into transcripts (written accounts of testimony). Then they demand that the parties stick to the points raised in the hearing, Aramburu said.

People don't realize that doors are being slammed because they haven't established certain points at the council hearing, Aramburu cautioned; he warned that people are waltzing through the process. Waltzers are destined to become wallflowers because the courts are marching to the drum beat of tighter controls. Tighter controls are intended to correct sloppy local governments.

From the preceding four cases Aramburu concluded that the state Supreme Court is getting fed up with finding city and county council decisions made "in a very sloppy fashion." Decisions sometimes are made at public hearings without sworn testimony; or decisions are made by people who have an ax to grind, Aramburu said. When the courts look at that process, they see nothing resembling due process, he asserted.

BEHOLDEN JUDGES

Aramburu sees land-use decisions resulting from political considerations. Even the courts aren't free of that characteristic. One textbook on zoning law says there are two theories on how courts make decisions. One is based on application of rules of law; the other is based on "stomach jurisprudence," meaning that judges find legal legitimacy to justify decisions made on an emotional basis. Two land-use authors disagree. They argue that judges are beholden to prevailing political thought for their jobs.

"No court is going to rule on a zoning case without knowing and calculating the political implications," wrote R. Robert Linowes and Don Allensworth in The Politics of Land Use Law. "To do otherwise would be to act irrationally in the political science sense, which judges can not do if they hope to stay in office." People are taught in college and law-school classrooms, and indeed told by many politicians, that the courts are isolated from politics and protected from interest-group and partisan influences, Linowes and Allensworth explain. Nothing could be farther from the truth; the courts are deeply immersed in politics, they argue. That is, judges who are beholden for their jobs are not isolated from political influence.

In conclusion, one question lingers. Why do the Petersons and the Parkridges assume importance in the tapestry of time? The answer is that the work of this building inspector and the impact of this court precedent let people know that government can be the good guy. Their work is necessary to diminish the news about the arbitrary actions of government—and arbitrary government plants the seeds of citizen apathy and distrust. Perhaps others will take a lesson from the occasional Galts, Laings, and Arlington Heights to build a better future.

10

INNOVATIONS FOR
POSITIVE GROWTH

The technology of tomorrow is here, alive in nooks and crannies across the nation. Builders and others in the vanguard point the way. The innovative beat the energy crunch; the imaginative use limited land supplies creatively; and the ingenious reduce red tape and build $12,840 homes.

Energy shortages, of course, already dictate building techniques. The field is a fluid one, though, as pioneers experiment and refine techniques. Some rely on short, wide buildings, feeling they are destined to replace slender, high-rise office towers. These squat buildings have fewer and smaller windows, each with dead air space between the panes to reduce heat and cold transfer. Even the old 1912 Weyerhaeuser office building has been retrofitted for energy efficiency, proving that new construction isn't necessary for efficiency. The 12-story building is heated largely by passive solar heat, by body heat, and by warmth generated from the computers inside. The Weyerhaeuser building, like others, is carefully insulated. A close-up view of several other building exteriors reveals that dark reflective glass and mirror glass are combined, reducing solar heat gain in the summer and making air conditioners less necessary. Exterior glass also reduces heat loss in the winter. A bronze "skin" on some exteriors produces the same result.

One building technique is simpler: put it underground. The structure doesn't necessarily have to be completely buried. Some schools and other structures are semiburied, surrounded with earthen embankments on outside walls. Undergrounding works. Underground warehouses are a marked contrast to the above-ground warehouses of earlier days, which consumed oil, mostly heating the feet of birds on the roof. Undergrounding relies on the principle used in root cellars in an earlier era. A similar principle, just as old, gives rise to windbreaks. In today's refined version, trees are planted around a home, with shrubs extending the barrier down to the ground. Windbreaks, like undergrounding, cut air infiltration, reducing fuel consumption. Windbreaks can make air conditioners unnecessary.

Building techniques using alternative energy sources are available. Most commonly, buildings are sited to take advantage of passive solar heating. More complicated are wind generators and methane-gas systems. Some people use wind generators (located away from the windbreak), plus solar panels, to generate heat and electricity. They collect rain water, then heat it by burning trash in a built-in incinerator. They may also use a Swedish Clivus Multrum to turn organic waste into compost. As a result, utility bills and energy consumption drop dramatically. One imaginative home-owner hooked up an "energy-cycle" to grind his grain, recharge batteries, and run the stereo. When he burned up calories on his energy-cycle, he created energy for those household items. Innovation is afoot in institutions, too. Monroe Prison is blazing the trail with a methane-gas heating system. Officials use sewage from prison dairy cows, producing methane to heat the prison. Composting is nothing new; only using the methane is modern. Methane might be called a by-product; the herd's main products are milk and cheese.

Conserving and creating even relatively small amounts of energy seem to be a sign of the times, from the energy-cycle to harnessing electricity from water-distribution pipelines. Large-scale subdivisions of tomorrow may borrow the way that one water district inserts turbines in water pipelines and mains. The turbines are connected to generators that generate electricity from the falling water. Turbines replace the old pressure-reducing valves.

The energy squeeze is also causing a shake-up of zoning practices. Ironically, two new ideas are bringing yesteryear back into fashion. Remember mother-in-law apartments? Now they're used to reduce the demand for rentals—Portland calls it Add-A-Rental. Furthermore, the American scene used to include mom-and-pop stores with attached living quarters. Now modern mixed-use zoning is coming into vogue, permitting construction of living units above first-floor shops, for example, thus reducing gas consumption between home and shopping or work. Various projects aim to cluster jobs and homes together. A fringe benefit, in some cases, is to shrink demand on land supplies.

A few modern-day pioneers are winning the skirmish with shrinking land supplies. One hopes that their land conservation techniques, detailed as follows, will help win the war, for mushrooming population is on a collision course with shrinking land supplies.

Stacking—Dagwood sandwich-style—and recycling are two proven remedies for the problem of dwindling land supplies. For example, a post office was built snuggled into the hillside and topped by several tiers of parking lots. Each level of parking was designed to relieve glutted streets. In another example, parking and warehouses under elevated portions of freeways utilized idle space. Another example of a land conservation technique appears to be fantasy, but it's fact. Out on 14th Avenue South and South 120th Street, tennis players and joggers occupied a three-acre park, constructed sandwich-style atop a buried water reservoir. Double duty meant avoiding using three acres for a park plus another three acres for a reservoir. Thus, three acres elsewhere were freed to help relieve the housing shortage. Dual use freed tax dollars, too, in terms of both land acquisition and maintenance (the water district didn't have to maintain land on top of the reservoir). The reservoir relied on a series of small domes in the ceiling for strength.

Recycling buildings proves successful, also eliminating unnecessary consumption of land. Perhaps the lesson with the largest impact stems from the schools. School districts across the land succumb to the syndrome of idle buildings, caused by population shifts. Empty buildings represent wastefulness, both of taxes and of land and materials. Waste can, however, be reduced, both before and after schools are built. Some school board members admit that new schools are not designed for flexibility in case of closure, despite experience with the shortsightedness of those who build existing nonflexible schools decades ago. New schools can be sited where they can have new lives as commercial centers and offices, particularly if the board chooses a site that is zoned commercial or multiple-family. Indeed, some schools do have new lives, once they have been declared surplus. Recycled schools are ideal for archive storehouses, county offices, and art centers. Chelsea and Moshier Schools, for example, have been recycled into county offices and a county art center. A third school, located in the shadow of an airport, was converted into an archive warehouse. In this case, the school district had vacated the building after winning a noise-settlement damage suit against the airport operator. The state leased the empty building for records and documents, instead of consuming land and materials building a structure to house the state archives. Recycling the building helped the county, too, because officials needed to move county records out of the high-rent, downtown courthouse.

Clearly, tomorrow doesn't have to be a bleak unknown. For even today, here and there across the national landscape, cases like those just described are emerging. Tomorrow is a game—one that the ingenious will win.

RED TAPE: SENTENCED TO DEATH

The challenge of tomorrow extends beyond building and siting practices. It includes regulation practices, more commonly known as red tape. Runaway regulation is not tolerated by the builders of tomorrow. In a "marriage" of builders and government, both parties proved that ingenuity can sentence excessive red tape to death. Their ingenuity is chronicled in a national report by the American Planning Association (APA). A composite of success stories from that report creates the following scene.

Developer Daniel confers with staff members from several departments in a preapplication conference. Then he submits two applications to a central desk, saving chasing all over. One application—for a routine project—whizzes through staff reviews, gaining a stamp of approval. The permit expediter shepherds the second request through, since it involves major change. Zoning Examiner Jones takes public testimony, issuing a final decision, subject to "call-up" (reconsideration) by the council. Even the second application doesn't take long, because it doesn't have to wait in line behind a backlog. The backlog was eliminated when the authorities revised the zoning code, reducing variance requests.

These streamlining strategies promise to be popular with developers, officials, and citizens; the need to streamline is one of the few issues they agree on. Indeed, who can argue with the streamlining results in Jim Conner's case? This developer saved $112,000 in interest fees when the county put his permit processing on a fast track, giving him a marketing advantage. Streamlining saved homebuyers money, too, because Conner passed on the savings. Without the speed-up, Conner's subdivision application would have taken 12 months to process; without the speed-up, he would have paid the lender interest for 12 months. With 6-month processing, the lender sliced the annual $225,000 fee to $112,000, Conner told a master builders' conference not long ago. As a result, the lender couldn't bill him for the remaining $112,000 for the remaining 6-month period.

In a marriage of mutual interest, the master builders and the county authorized Conner's pilot project, much as a city-homebuilders' working committee initiated streamlining in Kansas City, Missouri. Kansas City officials subsequently pledged to identify problem zoning cases early on, then see whether trouble spots could be streamlined, according to the APA report. No longer will Kansas City developers need to continue by-passing vacant city land, in favor of suburban land, to side-step permit obstacles.

The reason the marriage of builders to government works is that it benefits both mates. Government, the APA report finds, can save time and money by reorganizing the land-use process. One of the most promising ways to do this is to establish the post of hearing official, the APA report advised. Thanks to the establishment of a hearing-official post, Mountain View, California, saved $8,000 annually, according to the report. The windfall went to the Mountain View planning commission because it wasn't bogged down with routine cases. In another case, Lane County, Oregon, sliced processing time in half for more than 75 percent of its applications. Dual tracking saves time by speeding routine subdivisions and variances through staff decision making.

If the case load is too light to merit a hearing official, small jurisdictions can share examiners with nearby cities or counties. These part-time examiners can be objective, despite critics who claim they can't be. "It's a lonesome job," Examiner Robert Backstein said, happily. Parties don't try to bend his ear, prehearing, explained Backstein, a lawyer and part-time Pierce County examiner.

Two more illustrations of the use of personnel demonstrate the options available. Baltimore, Maryland, for example, uses a permit expediter to troubleshoot delay. Seattle, in another example, tightened up various departments in a personnel move. Unco-ordinated departments fuel developer complaints. The APA study sums up the complaint: "One department contradicts another. Environmental planners want to save all the trees, but the transportation department wants a full width cleared."

Hand in hand with better management of personnel is better management of information. One way to manage information better is to use computers. In booming San Jose, California, a computer logs applications, showing deadlines for action in zoning-type cases, according to the APA report. Computer print-outs show how long it takes to process certain types of applications, permitting elimination of bottlenecks. Computers whir away in Colorado, too. El Paso County, Colorado, computerized much of its record keeping and now processes an increasing workload with half the staff, the study reported.

According to the study, there are several keys to progressive government. "Model-T" governments can borrow these keys to help turn themselves into sleek, progressive governments. To start with, progressive governments simplify zoning-type codes, heeding the words of Governor John Spellman, who suspects building codes and standards need pruning. They shouldn't be wish lists, he asserted. Proliferation stems partially from environmental concerns. Some codes resemble overgrown lots; bulldozing and replanting are necessary because pruning won't work. Breckenridge, Colorado, completely replaced its zoning ordinance, thus opening the door to innovation. It uses a weighted point system, tied to a set of 250 development policies, according to the APA report. Put simply, the application will score points if it adheres to development policies. This simpler system reduces processing time, advocates say.

Also, at the onset, progressive governments should encourage informal meetings between staff members and the developer. One manifestation of that idea occurs in contract zoning. The government devises the contract after the developer appears informally before the council to present the proposal. In Des Moines, the contract might specify density, setback, and other requirements. Developers thus gain certainty, avoiding unnecessary architectural fees.

Finally, progressive governments eliminate duplicative hearings. The Phoenix, Arizona, planning commission, for one, holds a single public hearing on an application, the APA study stated. Sacramento County, California, for another, dropped hearing hurdles. A single hearing replaces four hearings on some routine cases. That was accomplished by devising a special-use permit system and by reserving rezone hearings for major changes, according to the APA study. For routine changes, developers consult a table to determine special uses within a district, then proceed to make application. This dual tracking benefits government, too. Sacramento County rezone requests have been reduced by 75 to 90 percent, and processing time has been cut in half, said John Vranicar, APA senior research associate.

Meanwhile, in the stampede to streamline, the National Association of Home Builders (NHB) has hired a full-time lobbyist to combat excessive regulation, according to Robert Sheehan, NHB research director. Curing overregulation isn't easy. Within the bureaucracy, there's tremendous resistance, lamented Gene Peterson, himself a county planning bureaucrat. Ben Thompson, director of the Tacoma Building Department, agreed. Thompson has seen agencies impede streamlining. He saw this when he pioneered a one-stop permit system. Agencies didn't want to lose their sovereignty, Thompson said, nor did they want to reduce staff when work was consolidated into a one-stop system. In implementing any cure, Sheehan cautioned, regulations shouldn't be relaxed haphazardly. "The patient [homebuilding industry] who is sick from overregulation may die from the cure," Sheehan warned.

Uncorrected overregulation forces builders to take matters into their own hands. Kingsley Hall, county plans examiner, described how one small builder solved energy-code entanglement—which provokes outrage from various developers—in his own way. He filed for 52 permits the day before the county code went into effect. In stockpiling permits, he saved $3,000 per home, since less regulation reduced cost.

Without doubt, regulations affecting energy and other areas can increase the cost—hence the selling price—of homes. Excess regulation, it is believed, creates housing that is not affordable. In some cases, rigid regulation (such as minimum square footage of house and lot) prevents construction of the smaller, compact homes that some feel the market desires. Here are two accounts of new compact homes, with the second accompanied by Jim Conner's message that builders and developers must be in the forefront to hit what the market wants. In both cases, work was necessary to find a flexible route through codes to permit compactness.

EVEN GENE FINDS THIS AFFORDABLE

Even county planner Gene Peterson ("I can't afford $50,000 and I'm not riffraff!") likes the price tag of this compact home. The three-bedroom home was built for $12,840. Construction techniques, not new technology, held down the cost of the Metcalfe, Mississippi, model home. Construction began with framing spaced at 24-inch intervals, instead of the 12-inch interval used in some areas. The home was designed to utilize the entire piece of wood from suppliers, reducing waste and custom cutting of rafters, joists, studs, plywood flooring, and siding, according to David Knepper of Rural America, Washington, D.C., the sponsor of the HUD project. Corners and intersections were connected with small metal brackets (drywall clips) rather than with extra studs, he said.

Success rests with smaller, simpler homes, Knepper said of his design for the 660-square foot home. One-bedroom plans, also suitable for vacation homes, contain 540 square feet. Space efficiency is achieved with built-in beds and dressing tables that do dual duty as desks. To compensate for the feeling of confinement, the home has a cathedral ceiling. Basically, the idea was to minimize costs for a starter home, knowing that the owner could later expand floor space, add closet doors, and replace no-frills kitchen cabinets. On the other hand, builders didn't skimp with insulation or with walls or windows, Knepper explained, adding that the home took advantage of passive solar heating. More elaborate heating systems, however, would increase costs in colder climates, since a wood-burning system was used in Mississippi.

If a private contractor built the model home, Knepper estimated, labor and materials would cost $18,000, since some labor for the model home was donated. Land expense, of course, would increase the selling price. Several private contractors are already aboard a nation-wide HUD program to build 50 counterparts. The housing industry will keep a close watch on consumer acceptance, according to the National Association of Realtors.

In other areas, realtors explored different alternatives. One was the "quad"—a fourplex of four attached units that resemble single-family houses backed into each other. Boston realtors sponsored a design competition for such a configuration. They estimated that the winning design could sell for $36,000 to $50,000 per unit.

A SECOND ACCOUNT OF AFFORDABLE HOMES

Like Knepper's compact home, Conner's economies evolved in the design stage, in terms of both the size and siting of the home and the size of the streets. In Conner's 150-unit subdivision, units ranged from 920 to 1,850 square feet. To create a feeling of spaciousness, the architect designed living rooms-dining rooms-family rooms that opened onto each other. To capitalize on available space in the 4,000- to 5,000-square foot lots, homes were sited to abut one lot line (this is the "zero-lot line" concept). The conventional lot contains 7,200 square feet; but, Conner said, the zero-lot line produced more useable free space on the opposite side yard than did the old, narrow setbacks. Units were oriented to the west or south to make maximum use of available sun—and to appeal to the energy-conscious consumer.

Conner slashed $8,000-$10,500 from the cost of each compact home. Conner's magic formula? He told a housing conference that using 40-foot right of ways was the biggest money saver. In the county, developers customarily pay for 60-foot right of ways in interior subdivision roads.

"How did you ever get the Department of Public Works to O.K. a 40-foot right of way?" county planner Gene Peterson asked with disbelief. "We started at the top with Director Jim Guenther," Conner replied. Conner's pilot project evolved out of discussions between the county and the master builders, so the county wanted it to succeed. The project's goal was "affordable housing." The 40-foot right of way found favor with Peterson. In his words, there's no reason to build a four-lane highway in the middle of a subdivision. Road costs were also reduced by the smaller lot sizes. Here's how it works: Smaller lots translate into narrower frontage. Less frontage means less street, sidewalk, and utility length. A 60-foot frontage draws a bill for 60 feet of street; a 50-foot frontage reduces the bill accordingly. The cost of streets, sewers, and other utilities is proportional to the street frontage, Conner explained.

Conner didn't end his war on costs there. Rather than build sidewalks on two sides of the street, he built single sidewalks. For safety's sake, he shunned locating them alongside the streets. Instead, interior walkways through green belts provide activity access and keep children's activities away from the streets, he explained.

Conner achieved more economies by avoiding concrete curbs and gutters. He replaced them with a thickened asphalt edge that directs drainage to storm structures. (Meanwhile, Tacoma has taken a step in that direction. The "rolled" curbs in Tacoma make more dollars and sense than the squared-off curbs in other areas, according to lawyer Tom Fishburne. When a curb is rolled, or sloped, the developer doesn't have to rip it up for a driveway when the house is sited.)

Efficiencies can also be designed into the transaction with the homebuyer. Homebuyers profit. It all unfolds from the fact that the county makes the developer dedicate a portion of land for open space. Conner dedicated one-third of the 29.25 acres to the home-owners as open space. Open space, however, can create a management burden for homeowners' associations; upkeep can be a burden. To minimize management, Conner sold under fee-simple ownership arrangements instead of selling condo ownerships.

Conner is convinced of the value of fee-simple ownership. He detailed the advantages to the buyer and seller: It means ease of finance for the developer and for the purchaser. Development, construction, and take-out financing may be arranged separately and in varying amounts. This allows flexibility in construction schedules to meet market demand and an opportunity to look for competitive financing rates. Buyers can either use the developer's precommitted financing or arrange for their own. Further, fee-simple ownership means all sales can be closed immediately without a requirement for presales of a percentage of the development. Also, the developer can sell lots to other builders to provide for a variety of housing choices and competitive pricing. For example, Conner said, he sold 40 of 150 lots to different builders. From another angle, fee-simple ownership means a multiplex may be sold to one owner, who can then offer the units for rent. Conner's subdivision was a mix of single-family, duplex, and triplex units.

FINANCIAL ASPECTS

Only the unschooled would overlook the impact of financial aspects on housing. Financial incentives and disincentives are tools that encourage affordable housing (more about that later). Conversely, the financial impact from speculators drives up prices. An example of the firewater of speculation is evident in one Federal Way case. Here, speculators collected a tidy $500,000 profit in one day. The 40 acres had been priced under $40,000 ten years earlier, then jumped from $1.3 to $1.8 million in a single day when sold for a proposed shopping center. Escalation couldn't help but hike surrounding property values, even before the shopping center was built; speculation begets higher property taxes for neighbors. To curb speculation, Dennis Derickson, Everett planning director, and Richard Haag, University of Washington professor and architect, called for antispeculation laws. They aren't the only ones who favor such laws.

In the hottest of the boom areas—like Washington, D.C., and Los Angeles—cries are going up for strict rent control, for limits on condominium conversion, and for antispeculator laws, Nicholas Lemann writes in the Washington Monthly. Lemann calls for tax incentives and disincentives to burst the real-estate bubble—and to swell housing supply. More supply drives prices down, said Lemann, a Washington Post reporter. His plan gets government into the act. According to Lemann, government should:

Shave the capital-gains tax break, so that profits realized on a sale will qualify for federal tax reductions only to the extent that the property has been improved

Slow the climb to more-expensive housing by stopping capital-gains breaks for plowing profits from a home sale into the purchase of a more expensive home. Instead, give tax breaks for plowing those profits into shares of a new business.

Redirect tax breaks on home-mortgage interest away from buyers of existing housing; give those breaks to buyers of new homes and rehabilitators of abandoned housing. Average interest rates over the life of the mortgage to encourage lengthy ownership.

Governor Spellman knows income-tax policy fosters home ownership because owners deduct mortgage interest, but, he went on, it should be complemented by giving tax incentives to builders, to investors, to create more affordable housing. "We should work together to see that change accomplished," urged Spellman, a veteran member of the National Association of Counties' Land Use Committee.

Furthermore, he said, the lender should be part of the strategy, a part of the solution. Insisting on innovation, Spellman challenged public lenders to make loans on mixed-use projects. These mix residential and nonresidential use in one geographical area or, to use another example, combine a home and shop in the same structure. The time has come for mixed-use zoning, zero-lot lines, and townhouse zoning, Spellman urged. Bill Palmer, planning director of Kitsap County, countered that developers tell him that it's difficult for them to "sell" mixed use to the financial community. In short, they can't get loans.

NATIONAL COUNCIL

The financial community will "buy" the pitch for mixed-use project loans on a broader scale if Harold Jensen gets his way. Jensen is a Chicago real-estate developer who cochairs the Council on Development Choices for the '80s. The council, cochaired by Arizona Governor Bruce Babbitt, is funded by HUD. The Urban Land Institute, a Washington, D.C., research organization, is working with the council.

Jensen doesn't just argue for mixed-use zoning per se. Instead, he traces a chain of interrelationships. To start with, he said, developers try to meet the growing demand for economical, transit-accessible housing, for developments that put people closer to shops and work places. Developers, though, buck obstacles in their efforts to satisfy the market, Jensen explained. Antiquated, single-purpose zoning laws are one roadblock, he contended. Zoning "is a throwback to the 1920s" when zoning was invented to protect homes from slaughterhouses and other offensive neighbors, Jensen maintains. Today, however, environmental laws make such zoning superfluous, he pointed out. Outmoded zoning laws, he claims, segregate housing types and commercial structures. "So we continue to make people drive across town to buy a loaf of bread or drive 15 miles to go to work," Jensen declared. Why not, he asked, try mixed-use zoning? Here are some examples of mixed use that have been springing up, here and there, across the nation.

Illinois Center, an 83-acre redevelopment project that will use surplus railroad land near Chicago's Loop. Planned are 7,700 residential units, almost 17 million square feet of office space, 1.25
million square feet of retail space, 5,500 hotel rooms, and 10
acres of park and riverfront esplanade.

Lowertown, in St. Paul, is envisioned as a mix of office, shops,
and apartments.

Harmon Cove, a 750-acre project in the New Jersey Meadowlands,
will mix townhouses, shops, offices, and industrial use.

Johns Landing, a 70-acre Portland project, will offer offices, retail
outlets, and residential use.

There are at least three tools that encourage mixed use: crea-
tion of a new zoning category; revision of tax policy; and education
to remove "mindsets" against mixed use, according to Jensen. Jensen's council suggested increasing tax depreciation allowances for
commercial uses in mixed-use projects that include housing. He
also calls for investment tax credits to encourage industry to locate
or invest in mixed-use developments, and revision of FHA multiple-
family insurance policies to allow use of FHA insurance for residential portions of mixed-use projects.

Another roadblock, Jensen asserted, results from America's
mindset that housing is the only investment that can ride the inflation
roller coaster. The common belief is that the most secure investment is a four-bedroom, two-bath house on a single-family lot in the
suburbs, Jensen explained. To protect their investment, he finds,
people resist townhouses or clustered housing "with prejudice, if
not as an anathema." Remove the barnacles of today's system by
conducting a major educational effort to convince local government,
citizens, and developers of the advantages of mixed-use development—but don't throw dollars at the problem by creating a new federal or state program, he warned, knowing that dollars come with
strings attached. He resists a dictated mandate from Washington,
D.C., as embodied in so many federal programs.

In this educational effort, Jensen said, the council should survey the nation for the best development models now evolving spon-
taneously, in the hopes that they'll afford inspiration and direction.
The council will also embrace such ideas as mixed development, including townhouses or apartments within walking or close commuting
distance to stores and work places, according to Jensen. It will also
call for in-fill (developing vacant lots in settled communities), he
added.

Jensen's council isn't alone in its thinking. Here's a case
where energy-efficient villages are espoused by a conglomerate.
The Central Newcastle Property Owners Association has mapped out

four villages on the 6,200 acres it holds in common. Each village, of about 600 acres, would contain townhouses, garden apartments, and single-family homes. The association has met with resistance from a leader of the Issaquah Alps Trails Club, and the Newcastle Community Plan citizen panel recommended villages only by a narrow 11-to-10 vote. One member summed up sentiment, saying he wants to see how one village works out before making a commitment to four.

Does the council's backing of in-fill find favor? Not with everyone; in theory, it sounds fine to build in already developed areas with existing utilities, said Jim Summers, a master builders' group leader. In practice, however, master builders' members find, primarily in the multiple-family sector, that the ground that's available is available only on maps, he explained. For various reasons, the property can't be developed, Summers said. Either the people who own it are unwilling to sell, or it has adverse topographic or soil conditions that don't allow it to be developed economically, he explained. Instead of in-fill, the affiliate's position is that the county should direct its efforts toward freeing land for development in outlying areas like Northshore, East Lake Sammamish Plateau, and Newcastle, said Summers, adding that he favors the Newcastle village plan.

In-fill is a key ingredient in the growth-management concept that is now in vogue. Growth management may put the brakes on sprawl, guiding growth into areas easily serviced by streets and sewers. Whether it can deliver the savings promised remains to be seen, but in various states, governments at state, regional, and county levels climb aboard the bandwagon of growth management.

Poised on the doorstep of the 1980s, government belts out a growth-management chorus: "conserve taxes, conserve land." Other land-use tunes today include: a military march for progrowth and antigrowth forces; a croon of conciliation for embattled residents and developers; oratorio from the courts for tightening land-use controls; and, finally, scattered about, a melody from the innovative individuals who march to their own drumbeat. They, too, are the builders of tomorrow.

FOR FURTHER READING

American Planning Association (APA), prepared for the U.S. Department of Housing and Urban Development. Streamlining Land Use Regulation. Chicago: APA, 1980.

This 74-page booklet summarizes streamlining strategies used by various cities and counties, giving a comprehensive, practical guide to reforms.

American Planning Association. Planning. Chicago: APA.

This monthly magazine is designed to keep those associated with planning abreast of current changes.

Babcock, Richard. The Zoning Game. Madison, Wis.: University of Wisconsin Press, 1966.

Known as the granddaddy of the land-use game.

Business Publishers, Inc. Land Use Planning Report. Silver Spring, Md.: Business Publishers.

This weekly newsletter contains capsule reports about federal opinion-leaders and issues and lists status of legislation germane to land use.

Fahey, Tim. Property Dynamics. Kirkland, Wash.: Tim Fahey.

A monthly publication that gives Pacific Northwest developers nuts and bolts data on population, rental ranges, and building permit activity. Look for real estate research counterparts in other jurisdictions.

Gardiner, John A., Theodore R. Lyman, and Steven A. Waldhorn. Corruption in Land Use and Building Regulation. Washington,

D.C.: National Institute of Law Enforcement and Criminal Justice, 1979.

These materials were analyzed in greater depth in Decisions for Sale: Corruption in Zoning and Building Regulations, by Gardiner and Lyman. New York: Praeger, 1978.

League of Women Voters of the United States. Growth and Land Use: Shaping Future Patterns. Washington, D.C.: League of Women Voters of the United States, 1977.

This pamphlet is the most valuable of several informative pieces, published by the league.

Linowes, R. Robert and Don Allensworth. The Politics of Land Use Law. New York: Praeger, 1976.

Doesn't pussyfoot around the issue of politics in land use.

National Wildlife Federation. Conservation Directory, 26th ed. Washington, D.C.: National Wildlife Federation, 1981.

An inch-thick directory that gives up-to-date names of leaders in public and private (citizen and environmental) organizations. Primarily designed for citizen activists and environmentalists, it may also prove of value to developers. The National Wildlife Federation also publishes a weekly update on conservation legislation called the Conservation Report.

The Urban Institute. Publications Catalog. Washington, D.C.: The Urban Institute.

This independent, nonprofit research organization, established in 1968, issues an informative catalog on The Urban Institute publications that cover topics ranging from land use to social issues.

The Urban Land Institute. Publications Catalog. Washington, D.C.: The Urban Land Institute.

This independent, nonprofit research organization, founded in Chicago in 1936, issues an informative catalog on its publications

that focus on land use. For example, the institute provided the
support staff for the report issued by the Council on Development
Choices for the '80s, co-chaired by Chicago developer Harold
Jensen.

(Also of note are the trade publications from master builders, realtors, architects and planners, as well as California State's appropriate technology publication.)

APPENDIX A:
GLOSSARY

Note: Glossary and zoning items are drawn from King County, Washington. They provide a roadmap for readers, who can take them to their jurisdiction and ask for counterparts.

CONDITIONAL-USE PERMIT   Is needed when owners want to develop property for a special use. Examples   To extract gravel, to establish a day nursery.

DENSITY   Number of units per acre.

PLANNED-UNIT DEVELOPMENT (PUD)   Permits flexibility within a zone. Example   To trade off between green space and density, up to a maximum density.

PLAT   A legally created lot or building site. To plat means to subdivide.

POTENTIAL ZONE   A second zoning, apart from existing zoning. Potential zoning recognizes the suitability of a location for a future type of use. It does not guarantee rezoning.

"P" SUFFIX   Prevents development from proceeding until the site plan is approved. Example   000-82-P.

SHORT SUBDIVISION   Four lots or fewer from a parcel of property. County administrative approval is needed to create a short subdivision known as a short plat.

SUBDIVIDE   Legally to create more than four lots from a piece of property.

UNCLASSIFIED-USE PERMIT   Is needed when owners want to develop property for a unique use. Example   A helicopter pad.

VARIANCE   An adjustment of zoning regulations for a property deprived of privileges commonly enjoyed by other properties in the same vicinity and zone category.

MAJOR ZONINGS

RS 7200   Residential single-family at 1 unit per 7,200 square feet.

RS 9600   Residential single-family at 1 unit per 9,600 square feet.

RM 2400   Multiple-dwelling medium density.

RM 1800   Multiple-dwelling high density.

RM 900   Multiple-dwelling maximum density (permits certain professional offices).

BN   Neighborhood business.

BC   Community business.

CG   General commercial.

ML   Light manufacturing.

APPENDIX B:
ORGANIZATIONS OF INTEREST

American Planning Association, 1313 E. 60th St., Chicago, Ill.
60637

Friends of the Earth, 124 Spear St., San Francisco, Calif. 94105

Land Use Planning Report, published by Business Publishers, Inc.,
P.O. Box 1067, Silver Spring, Md. 20910

League of Women Voters of the United States, 1730 M St., N.W.,
Washington, D.C. 20036

1,000 Friends of Oregon, 400 Dekum Building, 519 S.W. Third,
Portland, Ore. 97204

National League of Cities, 1301 Pennsylvania Ave., Washington,
D.C. 20004

National Association of Counties, 1735 New York Ave., N.W.,
Washington, D.C. 20006

National Association of Home Builders, 15th & M Streets, N.W.,
Washington, D.C. 20005

National Association of Neighborhoods, 1612 20th St., N.W.,
Washington, D.C. 20009

National Association of Realtors, 430 N. Michigan Ave., Chicago,
Ill. 60611

National Wildlife Federation, 1412 16th St., N.W., Washington,
D.C. 20036 (publishes an annual directory that lists organizations, agencies, and officials involved with resource use)

Sierra Club, 530 Bush St., San Francisco, Calif. 94108

Small Towns Institute, P.O. Box 517, Ellensburg, Wash. 98926

The Urban Institute, 2100 M St., N.W., Washington, D.C. 20037
(publishes books)

Urban Land Institute, 1090 Vermont Ave., N.W., Washington,
D.C. 20005

Many organizations issue newsletters.

APPENDIX C:
REZONING STEP-BY-STEP

Here is a thumbnail sketch of the main actors and elements in the zoning game. King County's pattern is given. This pattern applies in any area, although the names of the players vary somewhat. For example, a "planning commission" instead of a "zoning examiner" may hear a case.

DOCUMENTS

The county has a zoning code, which establishes regulations governing land use. The county's 1964 comprehensive land-use plan maps out use of the land and, in some cases, potential zoning. With the assistance of citizens, the county is forming community land-use plans for individual neighborhoods. The county council is the final, approving authority for documents. The Washington State Legislature passed the State Environmental Policy Act of 1971, which requires the "lead agency" (often the county) to prepare an Environmental Impact Statement (EIS) for those projects that the agency judges to have a significant adverse impact on the environment. All along the way in the overall process, lawyers, community activists, and organizations get into the act. Here are the main decision makers and agencies.

STEP ONE

An applicant applies for a rezone, building permit, conditional-use or unclassified-use permit (see the Glossary, Appendix A, for definitions), planned-unit development, subdivision, or variance from the county Building and Land Development Division (BALD). Public notice is given as follows:

Rezones, Unclassified-use Permits, and Planned-unit Developments. BALD sends the hearing date by first-class mail to property owners within a 500-foot radius at least 30 days before the hearing, according to Ed Sand, BALD director. The hearing is announced in legal ads, both in the county "gazette" (the Issaquah Press, in 1978) and in the affected area. For rezones only, BALD posts a 27- by 22-inch sign on the subject property at least four weeks before the hearing. Note: The file number (for example, 229-82-R) on the notification should be retained for identification whenever you communicate with the county.

Variances and Conditional-use Permits. BALD mails the hearing date to property owners within 500 feet at least 12 days before the hearing.

Subdivisions. BALD causes the applicant to post three signs announcing the hearing on the property at least 14 days prior to the hearing. Legal ads are run in the same manner as for rezones.

Building Permits and EIS Cases. There are no legal requirements for advertising, and any notices are done at the option of the developer, according to Dorothy Owens, deputy county clerk. The developer must post a copy of the building permit application on the site. EIS hearings are optional.

 Note: Items within the above pattern may vary from jurisdiction to jurisdiction. Nevertheless, the pattern can cue questions like:

How many days advance notice does the government give before a
 hearing?
How do notification requirements vary between rezones and subdivisions? What are the notice requirements for building permits
 and EISs? What, if anything, determines if an EIS hearing is held?
Is notice done via a letter or via a posted sign? Is the government
 or developer responsible for providing notice?
Does an obscure newspaper—like the Issaquah Press—print legal
 notices about coming hearings? Is there any way to get interested parties or groups on a government mailing list regarding
 coming hearings?
How do you find out the file number for the case at hand?

STEP TWO

 Interested parties call the county zoning examiner's office, asking to become "a party of record" to get pre- and posthearing reports.

STEP THREE

 BALD staff reviews the application, deciding if the project needs an EIS. Regarding the rezone or other matter under consideration, a staff recommendation to the examiner will call for denial, approval, or approval subject to conditions. Land-use plans are cited. A review sometimes comes from the county department of planning and community development, whose objective, according to a county handbook, is to propose policy, develop programs, co-ordinate activities, and carry out projects relating to housing and community development. This department handles community land-use plans.

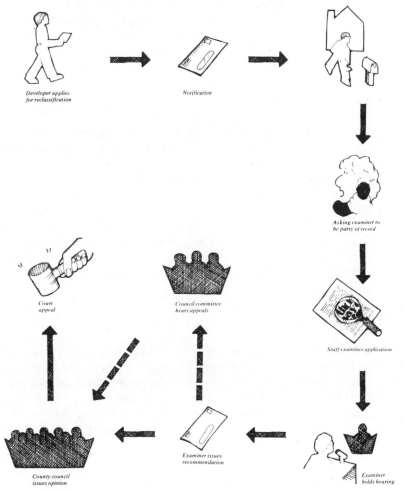

Developer applies
for reclassification

Notification

Asking examiner to
be party of record

Staff examines application

Court
appeal

Council committee
hears appeals

Examiner issues
recommendation

County council
issues opinion

Examiner
holds hearing

This illustrates the general path of reclassifications in King County, where the widely copied zoning examiner system was established in 1969.

STEP FOUR

The zoning examiner and BALD release BALD recommendations 14 days prior to the hearing. Picking up the report, rather than waiting for the mail, gives more hearing preparation time.

Citizens can testify by letter before a hearing or in person at the hearing conducted by the examiner, a single hearing officer. Weeks after the hearing, the examiner reports a recommendation (denial, approval, or approval subject to conditions) to county council members, in a hearing. They pass final judgment.

STEP FIVE

The examiner's opinion may be appealed to the council's parallel committees, Land-Use Appeals I and II. The committee's recommendation passes to the council for action.

STEP SIX

People appeal, at any time, to the county executive for a favorable statement. The county executive rarely vetoes a council decision.

STEP SEVEN

The county council exercises a great deal of power over decisions. This legislative branch is composed of nine council members, elected by district. The council can override a veto.

STEP EIGHT

Participants can appeal a council decision by filing in county Superior Court. The court's voice is also heard earlier in the process, in that precedent can influence action. In addition, the state Supreme Court's Appearance of Fairness Doctrine can invalidate a hearing conclusion, if either side meets with decision makers outside of the hearing. Impartial decision making is the objective of this Washington State doctrine.

APPENDIX D:
SAMPLE BYLAWS

Residents can save hours of research by adopting these bylaws, compiled from several sets. Or this sample can be used as a starting point for discussion, allowing residents to extract whatever fits their needs.

ARTICLE I: (Insert group's name here and in parentheses below.)

Section 1.   (   ), a non-profit (insert corporation or group), shall consist of property owners residing in (insert name of community).

ARTICLE II: Definitions

Section 1.   (   ) shall mean property owners residing between (insert street boundaries).

Section 2.   Members shall mean resident-property owners in good standing.

Section 3.   President, vice president, secretary and treasurer shall mean president, vice president, secretary and treasurer of the (   ).

Section 4.   Executive board shall mean the executive board of the (   ).

Section 5.   All references to president, vice president, secretary, treasurer, members, boards and committees shall mean the officers, boards, committees and members of (   ).

Section 6.   Elected officers of the (   ) shall mean president, vice president, secretary, treasurer and executive board members.

Section 7.   The use of masculine, feminine and neuter pronouns, and the singular and plural shall be used interchangeably.

ARTICLE III: Rules of Order

Section 1.   In all instances, when not inconsistent with the provisions of these bylaws, Robert's Rules of Order, Newly Revised, shall govern the conduct of all meetings of the (   ), the executive board and all committees.

ARTICLE IV: Quorum for Transaction of Business

Section 1.   Except as hereinafter provided, twenty (20) percent of the members authorized to attend and vote at any meeting of the (   ) shall constitute a quorum for the transaction of business.

Section 2.   Except as hereinafter provided, a majority of the members of the executive board and all committees designated by these bylaws shall constitute a quorum for the transaction of business.

Section 3.   At special meetings of the (   ), for the purpose of removing an elected officer, a quorum shall be fifty (50) percent of the members authorized to attend and vote.

ARTICLE V: Fiscal Year

Section 1.   The fiscal year of the (   ) shall be from July 1 to June 30, inclusive. All budgets, bookkeeping and audits of the (   ) financial affairs shall be on a fiscal-year basis.

ARTICLE VI: Election and Terms of Office

Section 1.   Election of the president, vice president, secretary, treasurer and executive board members shall take place at the December meeting of the (   ) during even-numbered years.

Section 2.   All officers shall be elected for a two (2) year term.

Section 3.   After the elections, new officers will take office and proceed with the orderly transition on Jan. 1 in odd-numbered years.

Section 4.   All appointments, committees, budgets, schedules, etc., in existence immediately prior to the election of officers shall continue to exist and function until Jan. 1, when not inconsistent with the provisions of these bylaws.

ARTICLE VII: President

Section 1.   The president is the chief executive officer of the (   ), and as such is responsible for all activities of the (   ).

Section 2.   The president shall appoint committee chairmen responsible for specific activities, with both the appointment and the specific activities subject to the approval of the executive board.

Section 3.   It shall be the responsibility of the president, subject to the limitations of the budget, to direct the allocation and apportionment of funds. Also, the president shall be responsible for the preparation and presentation of a finance report to be given annually to the membership at the end of the fiscal year.

Section 4. The president shall preside as chairman at all meetings of the (   ), when not inconsistent with the provisions of these bylaws. The president shall also preside as chairman of the executive board and at such other meetings as are appropriate to his office.

Section 5. The president shall serve during the period of time as prescribed in Article VI, unless his office shall sooner become vacant.

Section 6. Unless otherwise directed, all committees are responsible to the president.

Section 7. Administration of the affairs of the (   ) shall be vested in the president, subject to the approval of the executive board.

Section 8. The president shall have the power to remove from office any person appointed by him, provided a majority of the executive board approve the removal.

ARTICLE VIII: Vice President

Section 1. It shall be the duty of the vice president to assist and advise the president in promoting the (   ) activities and programs. The vice president shall exercise all the powers and perform all the duties of the president in his absence. In the event there shall be a vacancy in the office of president, the vice president shall perform such further duties as assigned by the president and other articles of these bylaws.

Section 2. The vice president shall serve during the period of time as prescribed in Article VI, unless his office shall be sooner vacant.

ARTICLE IX: Secretary

Section 1. It shall be the duty of the secretary to keep the minutes of all meetings of (   ) and of all meetings of the executive board. The secretary shall be responsible for all correspondence concerning the activities and programs of the (   ) and shall maintain a roster of members in good standing.

Section 2.   The secretary shall serve during the period of
                 time as prescribed in Article VI, unless the office
                 shall be sooner vacant.

ARTICLE X: Treasurer
Section 1.   It shall be the duty of the treasurer to keep appro-
                 priate records of all funds of the (   ). He
                 shall be the custodian of all funds, showing a com-
                 plete record of dues, receipts and disbursements,
                 and shall disburse funds only on the order of the
                 president and within the limitations set by the bud-
                 get committee.
Section 2.   The treasurer shall submit to the executive board
                 a monthly fiscal report, and such other fiscal re-
                 ports as the executive board may request. His
                 books within three (3) months of the end of the fis-
                 cal year shall be audited by an accountant selected
                 by the executive board.
Section 3.   The treasurer shall serve during the period of
                 time as prescribed in Article VI, unless his office
                 shall be sooner vacant.

ARTICLE XI: Executive Board
Section 1.   The executive board shall be comprised of the
                 president, vice president, secretary, treasurer
                 and three (3) elected executive board members.
                 The executive board shall have all the powers of
                 the membership of the (   ) between regularly
                 scheduled meetings, excepting those relative to the
                 election and removal of officers and the adoption
                 and amending of these bylaws.
Section 2.   The executive board shall meet regularly every
                 month at such time and place as it shall previously
                 schedule. Special meetings of the executive board
                 may be called by the president or by two-thirds
                 (2/3) of the members of the executive board on five
                 (5) days notice.

ARTICLE XII: Membership, Dues and Holding Elected Office
Section 1.   Resident property owners, as described in Article
                 II, Section 1, shall be eligible for membership in
                 the (   )
Section 2.   Annual dues shall be ($) per year, per house-
                 hold, and are due and payable no later than March
                 31 of each year.

Section 3.   To be a member in good standing, the requirements of Sections 1 and 2 of this article must be
met.

Section 4.   To be eligible to vote at all meetings and for election of officers or to hold office in the (   ),
the requirements shall be those governing a member in good standing in Section 3 of this article.

ARTICLE XIII: Budget Committee

Section 1.   There shall be a budget committee, comprised of
the following:

a) A budget committee chairman, appointed by the
president and subject to the approval of the executive board;

b) The president or his designee;

c) The vice president and the secretary;

d) One (1) member of the executive board, chosen
from the three (3) elected board members;

e) Two (2) members in good standing appointed by
the executive board;

f) The treasurer as an ex-officio member.

Section 2.   The budget committee, after receipt of a revenue
budget from the finance committee, shall prepare
an annual budget, which shall not be greater than
the revenue budget. The budget shall be in two (2)
parts. The first part shall consist of those costs
essential to maintaining this organization and the
second part, all other desirable activities which
shall not commence until the money is in hand.

Section 3.   The budget for the following fiscal year shall be
presented to the executive board on or before May
31 of each year. The budget shall be subject to review by the executive board and shall not be effective until approved by the executive board. Formal
updates of the budget, following the procedures of
Section 2 of this article, must be submitted to the
executive board on or before Sept. 30 and Jan. 31.

Section 4.   No expenditure outside of the budget shall be made
by the president or any member of the (   ),
unless approval has first been obtained from the
budget committee and the executive board. Transfer may be made by the treasurer from one item in
the budget to another after approval by the budget
committee and the executive board. Vouchers,
signed by the president or his delegate, shall be

required for all funds of (   ), nor shall the president approve expenditures not included in the approved budget without first obtaining the approval of the budget committee and the executive board.

ARTICLE XIV: Finance Committee

Section 1.   There shall be a finance committee comprised of the following:
a) Finance committee chairman, appointed by the president with the approval of the executive board;
b) The president or his designee;
c) The vice president and secretary;
d) One (1) member of the executive board, chosen from the three (3) elected board members;
e) Two (2) members in good standing appointed by the executive board;
f) The treasurer as an ex-officio member.

Section 2.   Subject to the approval of the executive board, the finance committee is responsible for the conception and planning of all programs to solicit funds to finance the activities of (   ). All funds raised in the name of (   ) shall be transmitted to the treasurer.

Section 3.   The finance committee, by March 31 of each year, shall prepare and transmit to the budget committee and the executive board a revenue budget for the following fiscal year; this budget shall include the anticipated general sources of funds and the approximate timing of the receipt of funds. Formal updates of the revenue budget shall be prepared and transmitted, as above, by July 31 and Nov. 30 of each year.

ARTICLE XV: Elections, Vacancies and Removal of Elected Officers

Section 1.   The president, vice president, secretary, treasurer and executive board members shall be elected in that order by (   ) in accordance with the provisions of Article VI and Article XII. A simple majority of those members in good standing present and voting shall be necessary for election. Proxy votes shall not be allowed.

Section 2.   (   ) shall have the power by two-thirds (2/3) vote of the members in good standing present and voting to remove from office any elective officer for cause, which in the group's judgment may be deemed insufficient. If it shall be intended to remove any officer, a meeting of the (   ) for such purpose may be called or convened through the procedures provided for in Article XVI of these bylaws. The officer sought to be removed shall be given full and fair opportunity to present evidence and argument in his own behalf.

Section 3. If a person filling an elective office shall die, resign, or no longer be a resident property owner or be removed from office under the provisions of this article, his office shall be declared thereupon to be vacant.

Section 4. If a vacancy shall occur in any elective office, the executive board shall meet within two (2) weeks after such occurrence and shall appoint a nominating committee to nominate to fill such vacancy. The nominating committee shall be composed of the remaining elective officers and the following, to the extent possible:
a) Chairmen of the budget and finance committees;
b) Three (3) members in good standing appointed by the executive board.

Section 5. Not more than twenty (20) days following the occurrence of a vacancy in any elective office, the president, or if his office is vacant, the vice president, shall cause to be scheduled a meeting for the purpose of filling such vacancy, providing notice of not less than seven (7) days and not more than fourteen (14) days shall be given. Such notice shall fix a place and time for the meeting. At such meeting, the president, or if his office is vacant, the vice president as chairman, shall preside.

ARTICLE XVI: Meetings
Section 1. All regular meetings shall be on the (insert when, e.g., every 90 days or the first Monday of every month).

Section 2. The president shall preside, or in his absence, the vice president shall preside, at all regular and special meetings, excepting those meetings where it shall be intended to remove the president from office. This being the case, the vice president shall preside.

Section 3.   Special meetings of the (   ) may be called at any time by the president or the executive board on ten (10) days notice; and shall be called by the executive board to meet within two (2) weeks of receipt of a petition therefore, signed by at least twenty (20) percent of the total number of members in good standing.

ARTICLE XVII: Amending the Bylaws

Section 1.   These bylaws may be amended at any regular or special meeting of the (   ) by a two-thirds (2/3) vote of the members in good standing present and voting, provided the proposed amendment or amendments have been submitted in writing to the president and the executive board ten (10) days prior to consideration at any regular or special meeting.

Section 2.   The executive board shall be responsible for the printing and distribution of the amendment or amendments to the membership at the next regular or special meeting.

These bylaws were reprinted with the permission of Concerned Citizens of North Hill Inc., the group which opposed construction of Hidden Harbor Motel, as detailed in Chapter 5. Jeanne Moeller, (206)878-4983, president, may be called regarding establishment of a community group.

APPENDIX E:
ENVIRONMENTAL IMPACT STATEMENTS

Development friends and foes must learn about EISs because these documents determine in many controversial cases whether development is permitted. An Environmental Impact Statement draft contains before-and-after traffic counts, data on soil and water run-off conditions, and more. It tells how to mitigate damaging impact. This information is compiled by the developer, who submits it to the county or city for final review. Decision makers ultimately evaluate the EIS, perhaps deciding that adverse impact can be mitigated. Then they may grant a building permit.

The EIS—child of the State Environmental Policy Act of 1971 (SEPA)—is controversial itself. The issues boil down to power: who has it, and do they misuse it? Power struggles occur in the legislature and in individual EIS cases. Legislation was introduced in 1979 to restrict the power of the protester. Lobbyists fought for developers' power to use their land. Environmentalists and some local governments pressed for strengthening SEPA. Several leaders urged ending alleged misuse of SEPA by protesters. Protesters delay projects by asking for an EIS, acting as a deterrent, causing officials to watch every dot on every i, asking for rehearings, asking the courts to correct alleged defects, and more.

Lawyer Jerry Hillis declared that "9 times out of 10, [the EIS is] used as a roadblock, violating its purpose of safeguarding the environment." Former Yakima Planning Director Fred Stouder agreed, charging that SEPA is being used for the wrong reason: to stop construction. This consultant refuses even to write EISs. Chuck Keenan, a business lobbyist at the Western Environmental Trade Association, summed up his complaint this way: time means money to developers. Ambiguities of SEPA can be used to delay a project beyond reason.

State Supreme Court Chief Justice Robert Utter concurred. "I see the act being used as a means of delay. People defeat a project by delay, rather than by its merits." The difficulty is that the legislature did not establish guidelines for the functioning of the act, Utter went on. Thus, for the first few years of court rulings, it was difficult for government agencies, builders, and developers who were trying to proceed in good faith, explained Utter, who wrote the first five cases under the act, sometimes in dissent.

Decision makers ought to uphold the spirit of the act, but let developers who are complying in good faith get a decision within "an economic time frame," Utter urged. To prevent undue delay, some others call for limits on SEPA appeals, restricting the challenger to one appeal before one court. Still another viewpoint comes from former state Senator Hubert Donohue, D-Dayton, who sponsored a bill in the 1979 session to make protesters post a $5,000 bond before they could challenge the adequacy of an EIS in court. Some termed this overkill.

Stouder described a Bellingham case that demonstrated the interplay of power. "One day, Holiday Inn people came in for a building permit for a site appropriately zoned. The neighbors became enraged," he explained. "The next day, the building division insisted that the inn needed an EIS. Who's to blame for that—the regulations or how they are administered?" Ultimately, opposing sides "made a deal. The developers said, 'We will make a contribution to your neighborhood by allowing use of our pool.' And neighbors came away saying, 'We got something.'" The arbitrary administration of new environmental laws worsens the war between developers and residents, asserted Hillis.

County EIS Supervisor Ralph Colby has worked to correct application of EIS law. He was concerned about the built-in propensity on the part of the developer's consultant to submit a biased draft. Colby recognized that the consultant wanted to be hired again. We hope to overcome the bias in existence now, he said, calling for, first, compilation of a list of eligible consultants by the county and, second, giving the developer three names from the list. After the developer hired one of the consultants, the consultant would work with the county on the EIS, Colby explained. The applicant would be treated just like any other citizen—objections could be submitted in a letter to be attached to the EIS, he added. (See Chapter 5 for EIS tips.)

Colby portrays an EIS as a teen-ager, subject to fatherly discipline. Actually, EISs are the grandchildren of the 1970 National Environmental Policy Act (NEPA). NEPA demands that public agencies prepare impact statements; SEPA tells private parties that they must prepare statements for certain projects. NEPA requires each federal agency to prepare an EIS for any major action that will significantly affect the quality of the human environment. Half of all NEPA EISs have been written for road building undertaken by the Federal Highway Administration; these statements have resulted in significant planning changes, according to In Productive Harmony, published by the U.S. Environmental Protection Agency (EPA). Changes, EPA finds, include increased landscaping, hiking and bicycle trails along roadways, and the integration of mass transit routes into highway corridors. The second largest number of NEPA statements has been prepared for watershed protection and flood control projects, In productive Harmony explained.

A number of federally sponsored projects have been suspended, thanks to NEPA, the EPA booklet stated. For example, because of numerous opposing comments on the statement, the U.S. Army Corps of Engineers canceled construction plans for a proposed 1,760-foot pier off Maryland's Assateague Island National Seashore. In another example, the U.S. Department of Health, Education and Welfare scuttled plans for the incinerator to handle Bethesda Naval Hospital waste when the EIS showed several preferable alternative means of disposal, according to In Productive Harmony. Generally, federal EISs must be circulated to agencies for review of building displacement, housing and congestion in urban areas, water quality, radiation, noise control and abatement, and other factors. Like local EISs, NEPA statements list any unavoidable adverse environmental effects and any alternatives that might avoid adverse effects.

TWO FEDERAL ENVIRONMENTAL TOOLS

Here's another situation in which, as with the NEPA, federal legislation spawned local application. The Coastal Zone Management Act of 1972 has triggered many state shoreline programs in the 31 states that border the oceans and the Great Lakes. Here's a glimpse of how it works in one state. Thanks to the act, the state got about $1.5 million in 1980, said Emily Ray, planner for the state Department of Ecology (DOE). Funding was split between DOE, including funding for six DOE positions, and local government. More than $600,000 went to local government to administer and enhance shoreline management, according to Ray. Money was spent on a variety of projects, from a coastal zone atlas (a data repository ranging from sand and gravel to water flows) to data collection on the proposed Northern Tier Pipeline. These data were intended to help decision makers evaluate projects. Money also went for a park and walkway in a Bellingham fish-rearing facility, which was a rehabilitated sewer-treatment plant. In addition, matching funds were provided for designing the 11,600-acre Padilla Bay Estuarine Sanctuary.

Perhaps the most notable aspect of the act is the new coastal energy-impact grant. To illustrate: Clallam County received almost $50,000 for impacts associated with the Satsop Nuclear Plant. It is part of $605,994 received by local entities in one year. Purpose of the impact grant is to help local government prevent, reduce, or mitigate environmental losses due to energy development.

Regarding a second federal tool, an observer may wonder what the Federal Water Pollution Control Act has to do with land use. It isn't easy to dig out answers from a couple of 100-page booklets of amendments. This act did provide funding for a study on the need to extend federal oversight to Lake Tahoe, Nevada. Eventually, a co-ordinated effort by several agencies produced more protection of the fragile ecology of the lake.

The act was also the linchpin in a Normandy Park case, in which homeowners sued the government for contaminating their lake. Government had constructed a "holding pond" alongside the road because run-off from the asphalt road needed to go somewhere. Homeowners claimed that the waste water drained underground and then into their spring-fed lake, damaging its quality. The state Supreme Court ultimately handed down a ruling in favor of the homeowners. Thanks to the opinion, an exultant Dee Pedersen said, fellow homeowners won't have to suffer from discharge from "Normandy Vista septic tanks that are overflowing into the street." Now, she said, government must play by the same rules as private parties and get a National Pollution Discharge Elimination System (NPDES) permit.

All parties, including Aramburu, who represented the homeowners, agreed that the opinion set a national precedent. The idea
of using a NPDES to eliminate polluted waters hadn't been used before because people thought that the act applied only to pulp mills,
he explained, adding that in fact storm-water run-off has as bad an
accumulative effect.

Just as court cases hammer out what federal laws really mean,
citizens hammer out whether accountability exists. Ann Widditsch
took a close look at whether the Federal Water Pollution Control Act
(FWPCA) took account of public input. Follow-up should be improved,
this state Ecological Commission member said after conducting in-
terviews with those who had provided input in cases involving the
FWPCA. People should know that attention was paid to their comments, and whether or not they made a difference, she said. She
noted that almost none of those interviewed knew what had been done
with their comments.

SAMPLE ENVIRONMENTAL IMPACT STATEMENT

The Boeing Corporation envisioned a $15 million corporate
headquarters, overlooking Sea-Tac Airport. Planners pictured international customers visiting the showplace and seeing sleek Boeing-
built jets taking off. Boeing's building, however, may never take off.
It wasn't engine trouble; it was neighborhood protesters. Boeing itself wasn't the enemy, though. Residents held up Boeing rezone approval, as if they were holding it hostage, bristled one Port of
Seattle representative. The port ran the airport and owned the land.

Ghosts haunted the still-unresolved case, which dragged on for
four years. They were the ghosts of homeowners who occupied the
30-acre site before the port condemned the land for open-space buffer. "Are there any legal or moral restraints on the port acquiring
land at a low price, then reselling it at an inflated price to commercial interests—essentially stealing it?" That was how resident Mark
Casebolt summed up community resentment. That wasn't the port's
intention, port officials reassured members of the community, but
murmurs of skepticism rippled across the crowd of 135.

The Boeing EIS, part of the application for a rezone, never got
into the condemnation issue in those terms. This EIS, however, contained community letters that spoke of a broken trust. Letters expressed little sympathy for the port's decision to amend community
land-use plans (to permit the headquarters). The port called the business park "a buffer" separating the airport and adjoining homes; yet
most define a buffer as green space.

The following excerpts illustrate what an EIS can entail.

FINAL

ENVIRONMENTAL IMPACT STATEMENT

FOR THE

PROPOSED BOEING COMPANY CORPORATE HEADQUARTERS FACILITY

KING COUNTY
DEPARTMENT OF PLANNING AND COMMUNITY DEVELOPMENT

PORT OF SEATTLE
PLANNING AND RESEARCH DEPARTMENT

Prepared Pursuant
To:

THE WASHINGTON STATE ENVIRONMENTAL POLICY
ACT OF 1971 CHAPTER 43.21c REVISED CODE OF WASHINGTON

SEPA GUIDELINES, EFFECTIVE JANUARY 16, 1976
CHAPTER 197-10, WASHINGTON ADMINISTRATIVE CODE

KING COUNTY ORDINANCE 1700
(KING COUNTY CODE 20.44)

John P. Lynch, Director
Department of Planning and Community
Development, King County

DATE OF ISSUE: December 30, 1977

DATE COMMENTS DUE: February 6, 1978

COST PER COPY: $5.00

Glenn V. Lansing, Sr. Director
Operations and Facilities
Port of Seattle

DATE OF FINAL: March 9, 1978

1

INSERT TO THE ENVIRONMENTAL IMPACT STATEMENT FOR THE
PROPOSED BOEING COMPANY CORPORATE HEADQUARTERS FACILITY

This insert is a statement of the present status of the proposed construction
site as described in the adopted plans of King County and the Port of Seattle.

Purpose:

The purpose of this statement is to clarify the role of this EIS in the context
of other projects, proposals, and issues affecting the west side of Sea-Tac
International Airport north of south 176th Street. The specific area involved
includes the western edge of the airport east of and adjacent to 12th Avenue
South, and the westside residential communities immediately west of 12th Avenue
South. The area extends from South 156th Way (formerly Renton-Three Tree Point
Road) on the north to South 176th Street on the south.

Background:

For over two decades, the Port of Seattle (the "Port") has been gradually acquiring more land and expanding the size of the airport. This process has resulted
in the acquisition and removal of a number of residential units and has created
a climate of uncertainty as to the future stability of remaining residential
areas in proximity to the airport. In an effort to clarify the future role of
Sea-Tac Airport and to determine how it and its neighbors could best coexist,
the Port and King County (the "County") jointly initiated a planning project
in 1973 to develop a coordinated area plan. This effort resulted in adoption in
1976, by both the Port and the County, of the Sea-Tac Communities Plan (STCP).

During development of the STCP, serious consideration was given to the concept
of Port acquisition, for airport expansion, of some of the residential property
(17 acres) west of 12th Avenue South, and to "converting", through the gradual
application of zoning-based techniques, much of the remainder of the westside
residential communities (as shown on the accompanying map) to higher density
residential and/or commercial uses.

Although the "conversion" approach had some support in the community, it became
clear that many of the affected citizens were opposed to this concept. Opposition was strongly expressed, especially from residents living in the lower elevation portion of the west side. Another segment, the so-called "hilltop" community comprising about 35 acres and slightly over 100 homes, was not opposed to
conversion of the west side in general, provided that it accompanied acquisition
of all of their property and not just half, or about 17 of the 35 acres, as had
been suggested at one point in plan development.

Because of a lack of firmly identifiable long-term airport needs for such land
and the expressed opposition, the adopted Sea-Tac Communities Plan designated
all of the west side residential community as a "reinforcement" area - meaning
that policies should emphasize upgrading and improvement of the existing single-
family residential character of the area.

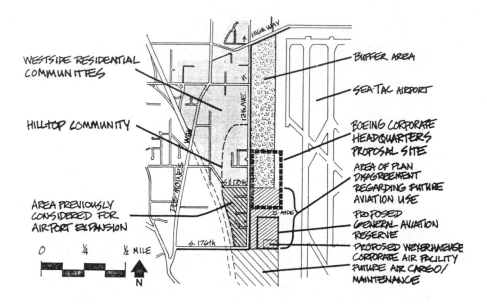

WESTSIDE RESIDENTIAL COMMUNITIES

HILLTOP COMMUNITY

AREA PREVIOUSLY CONSIDERED FOR AIRPORT EXPANSION

BUFFER AREA

SEA-TAC AIRPORT

BOEING CORPORATE HEADQUARTERS PROPOSAL SITE

AREA OF PLAN DISAGREEMENT REGARDING FUTURE AVIATION USE

PROPOSED GENERAL AVIATION RESERVE

PROPOSED WEYERHAEUSE CORPORATE AIR FACILITY FUTURE AIR CARGO/ MAINTENANCE

0   ¼   ½ MILE

N

At the time of STCP adoption, the need to adequately buffer the airport's existing and future uses through landscaping was recognized, but neither this nor
other provisions were identified in detail in the Plan. This resulted in continuing uncertainty among many residents of the west side community as to exactly
what might be the ultimate uses of the airport land adjacent to their neighborhood, and what impact such future uses might have on the desirability and stability of their area as a residential community. It was expected that further
environmental analysis and opportunity for public input would occur when specific
development proposals were identified for the airport's west side.

On December 19, 1977, the King County Council adopted the Highline Communities
Plan (HCP) which now augments the King County Comprehensive Plan and is the
official land use planning document used by all County officials and agencies
in reviewing and approving development proposals in the Highline area, which
encompasses the current proposal. The HCP adoption process afforded all interested and affected parties with a further opportunity for comment as to
the future development of the proposal site.

Introduction

Action Sponsor: The Boeing Company
                    7755 East Marginal Way South
                    Seattle, Washington 98108

Proposed Action: Community Plan Amendments, Zoning Reclassification, lease and other licenses and permits to allow construction of a Corporate Headquarters facility for the Boeing Company.

Project Location: The proposed development site lies on the western boundary of Sea-Tac International Airport east of 12th Avenue South, north of approximately South 173rd Street and south of approximately South 166th Place.

Nominal Lead Agency:	Joint Lead Agency:
King County	Port of Seattle

Responsible Official:	Responsible Official:
John P. Lynch, Director	Glenn V. Lansing, Sr. Director
Department of Planning and	Operations and Facilities
Community Development	Port of Seattle
W313 King County Courthouse	P. O. Box 1209
516 Third Avenue	Seattle, Washington 98111
Seattle, Washington 98104	

Contact Person:	Contact Person:
Harold Robertson, Planner	Ed Parks, Planner
Telephone (206) 344-7600	Telephone (206) 587-4630

Authors and Principal Contributors/Location of Background Data:

Environmental Analysis and Document Preparation - Wilsey & Ham, Inc., 631 Strander Boulevard, Tukwila, Washington 98188, (206) 248-2470

Technical Design Information - Skidmore, Owings & Merrill
One Maritime Plaza, San Francisco, California 94411 (415) 981-1555

Licenses Required: Zoning reclassification from RS-7200 to M-P, Comprehensive Plan Amendments (Highline Communities Plan and Sea-Tac Communities Plan), Draft and Final EIS approvals, grading permits, building permit; administrative approval of plans for access, landscaping, engineering and site plans, water and sewer hookup permits as required and construction inspection approvals.

Cost of Copies: $5.00; available at the County Planning Division; W-217, King County Courthouse. Make check payable to "King County Comptroller".

Date of Issue of Draft: December 30, 1977

Return comments to John P. Lynch by: February 6, 1978

Date of Issue of Final: March 9, 1978

2

Table of Contents

3

Recipients of the Draft EIS

Review Comments Received:	Date	Page	Response Page
Federal:			
Environmental Protection Agency	2/6	A-13	A-15
Department of Housing and Urban Development			
Federal Aviation Administration	2/6	A-16	A-22
State:			
Department of Transportation	1/12	A-2	-
Department of Commerce and Economic Development			
Office of Community Development			
Department of Ecology	2/10	A-5	A-9
Department of Fisheries	2/14	A-8	A-9
Department of Game			
Department of Highways			
Department of Natural Resources			
Department of Parks and Recreation	1/16	A-3	-
Department of Social and Health Services			
Office of Program Planning and Fiscal Management			
Regional:			
METRO			
Office of Environmental Management Division			
Port of Seattle			
Puget Sound Air Pollution Control Agency	1/27	A-4	-
Puget Sound Council of Governments	2/6	A-10	A-1:
Seattle-King County Department of Public Health	1/17	A-6	A-9
King County:			
King County Executive			
County Council			
Department of Budget and Program Development			
Building and Land Development Division			
Chief Deputy Fire Marshal			
Policy Development Commission			
Prosecuting Attorney			
Parks Division			
Planning Division			
Department of Public Safety			
Department of Public Works (Hydraulics)	1/20	A-7	A-9
(Roads)	2/7	A-14	A-15
Cities:			
City of Des Moines			
City of Normandy Park			

4

Summary of Contents of Draft EIS

THE PROPOSED PROJECT

The proposal is for a zone reclassification and comprehensive plan revision to allow construction of the Corporate Headquarters Office Facility for The Boeing Company, sponsor of the project, on an approximately 30-acre site located on the west side of Sea-Tac Airport. The site plan includes a headquarters building and accessory site improvements to be built as Phase I, and space for a future Phase II expansion building.

The Phase I project includes a two story building which would enclose approximately 95,000 square feet of space for offices and an additional 55,000 square feet for support facilities with parking for 235 cars underneath. Access roads would be constructed, an existing informal airport viewpoint and the Airport Surveillance Radar (ASR) structure would be relocated, and substantial regrading and landscaping of the site would occur. Approximately 200 employees would be assigned to the headquarters facility.

Although the sponsor has no current plans for further construction, space for a future Phase II expansion building is provided on the site. For purposes of potential impact analysis, it is assumed that the expansion building, if built, would be, at a maximum, similar in size to the Phase I building and would house a similar number of employees. Because of the present uncertainty as to future need for the expansion, the summary of its potential impacts is presented separately and follows the summary of potential impacts for the Phase I project.

ENVIRONMENTAL IMPACTS OF PHASE I

Geology and Topography

Topographic changes would occur on the building site due to grading and filling during construction. The intention of final design is to balance on-site cut and fill so that minimum fill material would have to be hauled to or from the site. Topographic changes due to the access roads would be negligible.

Soils and Erosion

Approximately 350,000 cubic yards of native soils material would be repositioned within the site. The soil is suitable for building support and for fill and backfill. The soils have a relatively low erodability, but an erosion potential would be created simply by the volume involved. This could be mitigated by completing grading during the dry season, by construction of temporary holding ponds as required and by landscaping immediately upon completion.

6

Hydrology

Since the total area of impervious surfaces will not be significantly changed, preliminary indications are that there would be little or no impact on water quality or rate of storm water runoff. Detailed engineering plans and runoff calculations have not been completed but will be required prior to issuance of grading and building permits.

Vegetation and Wildlife

Most existing vegetation would be removed from the building site and replaced by trees, shrubs and lawns. Most wildlife would be displaced during construction. Upon completion of the project, wildlife would return to approximately the same population levels but species diversity may be slightly decreased. No rare or endangered species occur on the site.

Air Quality

There would be a temporary increase in dust levels during construction. Long-term additional air pollutants would be negligible and indistinguishable from existing levels and sources.

Noise

There would be no long-term increase in existing levels of noise due to the building or related traffic. There would be a temporary increase in Noise Exposure Forecast (NEF) to approximately 42 from the existing 37 along 12th Avenue South during construction. NEF is the standard descriptor that was used in the Sea-Tac Communities Plan studies for development of airport noise remedy programs.

Natural Resources

Typical amounts of non-renewable resources such as sand, gravel, cement, steel, aluminum, and glass would be consumed by construction. The site would be committed to the proposed use for the foreseeable future.

Light and Glare

The glass exterior will reflect light. This would not pose a safety hazard to pilots as they would not be looking directly into the reflection when landing or taking off. Reflection would occur off-site only during very low sun angles on clear days, but would not significantly affect adjacent land uses.

Land Use

The site is zoned and, until 1972, was used for single-family residences. It was purchased by the Port of Seattle and converted to an open space buffer for the airport. The project would result in a local change in land use as identified in the adopted Highline Communities Plan, Sea-Tac Communities Plan and zoning. The project is not expected to encourage any change in surrounding land uses, but could help to stabilize existing nearby residential uses.

7

Population

The project would not have significant impact on population. It is not anticipated that many employees would relocate their residences after completion.

Housing

The project is not expected to have a significant impact on the market demand for housing in the adjacent residential area.

Transportation

Approximately 900 vehicular trips would be generated daily to or from the site. This would result in an insignificant impact to traffic on South 188th Street and other major arterials. The impact on South 156th Way (formerly Renton Three Tree Point Road) would be minor but could result in temporary minor congestion at nearby intersections during peak flow periods.

Public Services

Public services are adequate for the proposed project. However, formal agreements would be necessary between the Port of Seattle and the local Police and Fire Departments to clarify responsibilities.

Energy

The building would consume an average of 44,000 therms of natural gas yearly for heating and cooking purposes. Approximately two million kw hours of electricity would be consumed yearly on an average for cooling, lighting and machinery.

Utilities

Adequate telephone and electrical service is available and would be brought to the project boundary underground from existing systems. All other utilities would be brought to the project boundary by the Port of Seattle from existing Sea-Tac airport systems. Existing or planned utilities systems are adequate to handle the proposal.

Aesthetics

The building would be visible from the east, partially visible from 12th Avenue South and from greater distances to the west. It would be compatible with other structures around the airport. Landscape plans for the site would partially screen the building from the view of homes to the west by a berm and planting.

8

ENVIRONMENTAL IMPACTS OF PHASE II

The Phase II expansion building, if built in the future, would be similar to the Phase I building in size, occupancy and exterior architectural treatment. Because construction of Phase II would affect only a small portion of the site and would commence after the entire site has been initially rezoned, graded and landscaped in Phase I, additional impacts to most environmental elements would be minor. No significant impact would be anticipated to: Geology and Topography, Soils and Erosion, Hydrology, Vegetation and Wildlife, Land Use, Risk of Upset, Population and Housing, Public Services, Aesthetics, Recreation or Archeology/History. Elements which may experience potential impacts are as follows:

Air Quality

Temporary increase in dust levels during construction. Long term additional air pollutants would be negligible and indistinguishable from existing levels and sources.

Noise

Temporary increase in NEF level during construction as in Phase I. No long-term increase in NEF levels due to the building or related traffic.

Light and Glare

Sunlight would be reflected from the building's glass surfaces, but because the building would be more heavily screened by vegetation than the Phase I building, it would be even less likely to produce adverse reflection impacts.

Natural Resources

Typical amounts of non-renewable materials would be consumed by construction.

Transportation

Similar to Phase I, the expansion building would generate approximately 900 vehicle trips per day. Other than minor increases in peak hour congestion on the south access road and at intersections North and South of the site, traffic impacts should be insignificant.

Energy

The building would consume an average of 44,000 therms of natural gas yearly for heating and cooking purposes. Approximately two million kw hours of electricity would be consumed yearly on an average for cooling, lighting and machinery.

9

<u>Utilities</u>

Adequate utilities are available and would be brought to the site during
Phase I construction. Existing or planned utilities systems are adequate to
handle demand from the expansion building.

SUMMARY OF ALTERNATIVES

No-Action

Disapproval of the plan amendments or rezone would direct the sponsor to an
alternative site and retain the currently proposed site as an undeveloped
open-space buffer.

Alternative Sites

The sponsor with its architect, Skidmore, Owings and Merrill has seriously
considered five potential sites. The primary considerations in selecting
a site were architectural potential, corporate identity, expansion capability,
community acceptance, zoning compatibility, traffic impact, air quality
sensitivity, utility availability and soil conditions. The proposed site was
determined by the sponsor to be the most favorable considering all factors.

Alternative Use for Proposed Site

A portion of the proposed site is currently being used informally as a viewpoint and is recommended for development as a viewpoint park by the Sea-Tac
Communities Plan. The Highline Communities Plan designates the north and south
portions of the site as "Airport Open Space" and the central portion as "Parks
and Recreation." Potential alternatives uses for the site include landscaping
and maintenance of the open space buffer, development of the viewpoint park,
development for aviation uses, and development for other non-aviation commercial
uses. Uses other than open space or recreation would also require plan amendment and possibly rezoning.

10

POSSIBLE MITIGATING MEASURES

Traffic impact on South 156th Way would be mitigated by directing the majority of employees and all service traffic to use the south access road.

The visual impact to the westside communities would be mitigated by landscaping including the proposed berm and tree plantings.

The viewpoint would be relocated to an alternative site.

Erosion potential would be mitigated by scheduling major earthwork during the dry season, by construction of temporary holding ponds and by landscaping immediately upon completion.

Dust impact could be mitigated by watering the site during construction as needed.

Helicopter noise impact would be mitigated by directing approaches and departures to the east or south whenever possible.

REMAINING ADVERSE IMPACTS

Slight erosion potential during construction.
Removal of natural vegetation.
Minor local air pollution due to increased vehicular activity.
Minor noise impacts due to vehicular activity.
Increased traffic on secondary and primary arterials.
Partial visibility of the upper portion of the building from westside residences, particularly until landscaping matures.
A slight increase in sanitary sewage delivered through the Sea-Tac system to the Des Moines sewer system.

11

Existing Conditions, Environmental Impacts and Mitigation

▓ Elements of the Physical Environment

GEOLOGY AND TOPOGRAPHY

Existing Conditions

In general, the site slopes down approximately 20 to 30 feet from the flat airport surface on the east to 12th Avenue South on the west. The northern portion has been graded to create a large, nearly flat retention pond. The retention pond is surrounded on the north and west by a berm which drops steeply to the north and to 12th Avenue South on the west.

The central portion of the site rests on a bench approximately 20 feet above the airport surface. This raised bench is the site of an informal airport viewpoint and is the location for the proposed headquarters building. The bench slopes gradually down to 12th Avenue South on the west.

Existing topography and proposed changes to topography can be seen in Figure 7. The site is underlain by compact, impermeable, unsorted drift called Vashon Till. Road cuts along 12th Avenue South expose a typical random mix of clays, sands, gravels and boulders. Granite boulders exposed on the surface of the site are assumed to be remnant glacial erratics.

The unsorted drift, or till, is very hard, stable and resistant to erosion. However, once loosened by construction activity, the material becomes subject to erosion unless stabilized by vegetation or other means. It forms a stable base well suited to building foundation support and is generally insensitive to seismic disturbance. Much of the area that would be the subject of major grading activity has been previously graded and covered by building foundations and pavement. All buildings were removed a few years ago and only the access roads and the 1.2 acre abandoned tennis courts shown on Figure 7 remain.

Environmental Impact

Impacts to geology and topography would be limited to the specific project site. Grading, cutting and filling would cause a local change to the topography. The primary purposes of grading are to improve the aesthetic appearance of the building site, create a reflection pond and to screen the project from the westside residential communities by a berm. The project would result in negligible impact on surficial and subsurface geology at the site.

22

174

WILDLIFE

Existing Conditions

The wildlife of the site reflects the varied vegetational patterns. A variety of bird species was observed during site visits indicating a wildlife community typical of partially developed suburban areas.

The site is one of the several loosely connected, semi-natural, open spaces surrounding the airport. The combination of individual open spaces work together to support many species that probably could not survive on one individual site. For example, a red-tailed hawk, a sparrow hawk, and evidence of a coyote were observed on the site. All of these species range outside of the site daily. Only smaller birds and mammals would rely entirely on the project site to provide suitable habitat.

Within the site, there are several habitat types. These include dry grassland, brushy thickets, broadleaf forest, the mixed park-like habitat of scattered trees, shrubs and grass, and a small freshwater pond and marsh resulting from the artifically created retention pond.

No rare or endangered species are known to occur on the site. The site does not provide any unusual wildlife habitat.

Small flocks of crows (4-6) and starlings (10-20) were observed on the site and are indicative of the problems the airport has had with these species. Very large flocks occurring near the runways create safety hazards to aircraft. This has occurred particularly near the south end of the airport where a large habitat area of young alder and blackberry exists. It is about a mile and a quarter south of the proposal site.

Environmental Impact

During construction, both small and large animals would be displaced from the site. Although landscaping programs in the adjacent buffer areas may increase their ability to sustain some of the displaced wildlife, some reduction in numbers would be expected. This would be a temporary condition and, once construction and landscaping are completed on the site, both large and small animals would be expected to return fairly quickly. The species present have demonstated a tolerance of human activity and only a minor amount of habitat would be permanently lost.

32

175

Depending on the landscaping, wildlife diversity and populations may change slightly. The marsh habitat around the retention pond would be eliminated and an open pond habitat would be created by the proposed relfection pond. The proposed access roads would slightly reduce the amount of potential habitat, and the roads, fences and building would create barriers to the movements of small animals.

The landscaping changes proposed by the Port and by the sponsor could make the buffer areas more productive for wildlife. This might occur for two reasons: first, the vegetation itself will probably be more productive with management such as fertilizing and mowing. Second, the variety of habitat types and the "edge effect" between differing habitats would be increased. This should result in slightly increased populations and numbers of species.

Increased wildlife populations due to future landscaping projects, both on the proposed site and in the adjacent buffer areas, hold the potential for a secondary negative effect on airport operations. The possibility of creating a roost for large numbers of blackbirds, starlings or crows, thereby increasing a potential safety hazard to aircraft, must be considered.

Three points are significant in this consideration. First, the present roost near the south end of the airport is a large, homogeneous area of young alder and blackberry. Second, the west side in the vicinity of the proposed project is apparently not attractive now as a roost for large numbers of birds. Third, the proposed landscaping plans will not significantly change the mixed pattern of vegetation that currently exists. Thus, although it is not possible to state for certain, the proposed landscaping project probably will not create new roosts for large flocks of birds.

Mitigating Measures

Complete landscaping and maintenance of the berm and buffer areas in a seminatural condition would off-set the minor loss of habitat area.

If the project landscaping were to become a roost for large flocks, successful mitigating measures to control the numbers of birds are available. The U. S. Fish and Wildlife Service could provide technical assistance with the development of a roost control program.

33

NOISE

Existing Conditions

Man's response to noise is determined by the sound level emanating from the source of noise and the frequency spectrum of the sound. Noise intensity represents the level of sound which is weighted in accordance to the apparent loudness perceived by an average human observer. This number is expressed in "A"-weighted decibels and is written as dBA.

Noise intensity covers such a broad range that it is measured logarithmically and analyzed based on statistical averages. An average of an A-weighted sound level measurement is a measure of the mean acoustical energy level and does not readily account for the annoyance associated with loud sounds of short duration. Steady noise levels are rarely observed, and because of the time-varying characteristics of environmental noise, it is necessary to provide a statistical descriptor which indicates a dBA level and the percentage of time this level will be exceeded. The descriptor is designated by L, and L_{10} indicates the sound level in dB that will be exceeded 10% of the time. The "average" sound level is designated by L_{50}.

The Washington State Department of Ecology has specified regulations relating to maximum environmental noise levels. They have classified various areas or zones and established maximum permissible noise levels. These "EDNA's" (Environmental Designation for Noise Abatement) are classified as:

a) Residential areas - Class A EDNA
b) Commercial areas - Class B EDNA
c) Industrial areas - Class C EDNA

The maximum permissible noise levels for these zones are shown in Table II. These are the same levels used in the King County noise ordinance.

177

TABLE II*

NOISE LIMITATIONS

EDNA OF NOISE SOURCE	EDNA OF RECEIVING PROPERTY		
	CLASS A	CLASS B	CLASS C
CLASS A	55 dBA	57 dBA	60 dBA
CLASS B	57	60	65
CLASS C	60	65	70

*WAC 173-60

Between the hours of 10:00 PM and 7:00 AM the noise limitations of the foregoing table shall be reduced by 10 dBA for receiving property within Class A
EDNA's. These noise levels may be exceeded on the receiving property by 15
dBA for 1.5 minutes, 10 dBA for 5 minutes, 5 dBA for 15 minutes for any one
hour, day or night.

Since the majority of vehicular traffic on arterials and highways regularly
exceeds the standards promulgated in Table II, an additional set of standards has
been established for motor vehicles and is shown in Table III.

TABLE III*

MOTOR VEHICLE NOISE PERFORMANCE STANDARDS

VEHICLE CATEGORY	35 MPH OR LESS	OVER 35 MPH	MANUFACTURED AFTER 1975+
Motor vehicles over 10,000 lbs. GVWR or GCWR	86 dBA	90 dBA	86
Motorcycles	80	84	83
All other motor vehicles	76	80	80

+Added to Final EIS per response from Department of Public Health
*WAC 173-62

38

178

One of the major problems associated with activity in the vicinity of the airport is the noise levels created by jet aircraft activity. The Port of Seattle
and King County have completed several studies which are on file for those who
want detailed information on airport vicinity noise.

One noise study was conducted by Mr. Hugh Parry, noise consultant to the Port, to
determine the potential impact of general aviation facilities, including
corporate-size aircraft, on the west side of the airport. The area studied is
immediately south of this proposal site. As part of the study, noise readings
were taken along 12th Avenue South. The average (L_{50}) noise levels are shown
in Table IV.

TABLE IV

EXISTING (L_{50}) NOISE LEVELS ALONG 12TH AVENUE SOUTH

dBA

LOCATION		SOURCE		
	AUTOS	PROPELLER TAKE-OFFS	AIR CARRIER	AMBIENT
12th Avenue South and South 176th Street	64	58	67	42
12th Avenue South and South 170th Street	69	67	77	44

Noise levels are higher at South 170th and were higher because the microphone
was closer to the source for automobile generated noise. Aircraft noise was
higher at South 170th because of the elevation difference between the road
and the airport runways. South 176th Street was about 50 feet lower and below the line-of-sight of the runways.

Airport noise has often been assessed using a cumulative noise scale called
Noise Exposure Forecast (NEF) which incorporates other local noise contributors
in addition to aircraft operation noise. Although the NEF method has the
limitation of not relating directly to or reflecting ambient levels as measured
in dBA, it is considered a useful method for the prediction of future noise
levels. The proximity of the proposal site to Sea-Tac Airport suggests that

39

179

In order to estimate the noise impact of the helicopter on the surrounding community, the aircraft that will actually be used was run through a series of take-offs and landings directly from the north, south, east, and west. Simultaneous noise readings were taken at two locations. Site A was at 170th Street and 12th Avenue South and Site B was at South 168th Street and 8th Avenue South. An observer, without a noise meter, was stationed at Site C; South 160th and 12th Avenue South during the test.

Noise readings were taken with one General Radio and one Quest Type II sound level meter. The meters were calibrated just prior to use. Meters were set on slow response. Weather was overcast with no wind. Temperature was about 45°F. Readings were taken on November 8, 1977 between 1:45 and 2:15 PM. A reading was taken every ten seconds throughout the monitoring period. Data are shown in Table VI.

TABLE VI
SOUND LEVELS DURING HELICOPTER SIMULATION TESTS

Site	dBA				
	Max	L_{10}	L_{50}	L_{90}	Min
A South 170th and 12th South	78	62	54	47	40
B South 168th and 8th South	80	66	50	45	43

Sources of sound at Site A included, in addition to the helicopter, other aircraft take-offs and landings, passing traffic and children playing. At Site B, the primary sources of noise were passing cars and trucks with occasional noise from an airplane.

The impact of the helicopter flights from the various approach directions are shown in Figure 10. The change in noise levels as discrete helicopter operations events and their durations are shown. The average noise levels at Site A are shown for comparison purposes.

The figure shows that as the helicopter takes off or lands, there is an increase in the noise levels. The amount of increase is dependent on the approach direction in relation to the monitoring stations. The East and South approaches were discernible at Site A but only very slightly above average noise levels. The North approach showed a slightly greater noise level. The West approach was the most significant in terms of community impact because it flew right over the monitoring stations and the houses.

Duration of perceivable noise from any take-off or landing of the test helicopter was less than one minute in all cases for any approach direction.

The observer stationed at South 160th and 12th Avenue South noted that the greatest noise occurred during the North approach. Noise levels here approximated landing noises of air carrier approaches from the North. The West approach was perceived here also, but was quieter than local auto traffic. The East and South approaches were not discernible above ambient noises at this location.

Based on the simulation tests it appears that an East or South approach creates the least impact and would be perceived by the fewest people in the community. The North approach has a somewhat higher impact and the West approach has the most significant impact. Use of the East and South approaches should not create a significant noise impact in the community. These operations would usually be barely perceivable in the context of airport operations. Helicopter flights as proposed by the sponsor would not significantly increase NEF levels.

Mitigating Measures

The potential impact of helicopter noise can be minimized by controlling the direction of approaches to and take-offs from the site. The sponsor's intent is to utilize the eastern approach almost exclusively. This would reduce helicopter noise to a level barely discernible in residential areas. When air traffic conditions necessitate, the southern approach would be the next best alternative, and the northern approach should be used only if the other two are unavailable. Flights over the west side residential areas, which would produce the only significant potential impact, should not be permitted.

Mitigating measures that can be used to reduce the potential annoyance from construction noise include:

1) Limiting the use of noisy equipment to daylight hours.
2) Employing proper maintenance and operation of up-to-date equipment.
3) Completing installation of the proposed berm early in the construction sequence to partially shield later construction noise.

45

LAND USE

Existing Conditions

Existing Land Use:

The proposed building site is vacant at the present time. The area was previously occupied by houses and a private tennis facility which were removed
after the Port of Seattle acquired the property in the 1960's. The only
current active use is an informal airport viewpoint and access road. A
1.2 acre paved area near the center of the site is a remnant of the abandoned tennis courts. Existing site features are noted on the April, 1977
aerial photo in Figure 11.

Sea-Tac Airport lies immediately east of the site, and the Airport Surveillance
Radar (ASR) Tower is located approximately on the eastern edge of the proposed
building site. Land to the north has been acquired by the Port of Seattle
over the last several years and will soon be re-landscaped as a buffer area
between adjacent residential areas and the airport. All residences have been
removed from this area.

The Airport Surface Detection Equipment (ASDE) Tower is located on the large,
flat, grassy area near the southeast corner of the site, and to the southwest
of this tower is a 15-acre reserve area proposed by the Port of Seattle for
future general aviation use. This reserve area and its proposed development is the
subject of a separate EIS which is being circulated by the Port of Seattle.

To the west, across 12th Avenue South, is an established residential area
known as the "Westside Residential Community" which is a part of Burien
(unincorporated). The westside community is a diverse, single-family residential area which contains a variety of housing densities and ages. Several
clusters of 5 to 20 year old suburban homes are interspersed with numerous,
mostly older, more rural style homes on one and one-half to 4 acre plots.
Many of these larger lots are partially used for small-scale agricultural
activities. Crops such as corn and sunflowers can be seen, and several
horses, goats, and some domestic fowl are kept in the area. The westside
area is approximately 80 percent developed. The corridor for the extension
of SR 509 cuts diagonally through the area, and completion of this freeway
will provide a definite western boundary to the community.

48

The future of the westside community as a single-family residential area has been uncertain for a number of years. This uncertainty has been created by the intrusion of the SR 509 freeway corridor and by the land acquisition activities of the Port of Seattle related to expansion of Sea-Tac airport. Some residents of the area have indicated that the uncertain future has depressed land values for a number of years, but that things have begun to improve in recent months.

Contacts with several realtors in the local area indicate a general consensus that housing values are somewhat lower here than for comparable units in other areas, but that prices are increasing along with regional trends. Signs of uncertainty are indicated by a higher than average number of homes listed for sale during the past six months, and by a gradual increase in rental units. The unclear future of the westside area is seen by some realtors as a negative factor in the housing market, but the area's proximity to the airport and concern about noise is probably the main factor which discourages many potential buyers. The realtors are aware of the Sea-Tac Communities Plan and the subject proposal but are not sure, as yet, what impact these may have on the area. The most positive trend appears to be a recent improvement in confidence shown by local mortgage companies. Some of these familiar with the area are relaxing their down payment requirements, and conventional loans are becoming easier to secure in the westside areas.

Existing Zoning:

The site and most of the land for some distance around is designated RS-7200, a King County zone which allows basically single-family detached dwellings up to a density of about 4 units per acre. The site, along with all land east of 12th Avenue South, is currently in public ownership as part of Sea-Tac airport. Land owned by the Port of Seattle is not subject to County zoning regulations if used for airport related activities.

Since the proposal would involve a private non-airport use, County zoning controls will apply to the site and, therefore, a change in zoning designation from RS-7200 to Manufacturing Park (M-P) would be required to allow construction of the proposed facility. The M-P zone permits business and professional offices and is intended to establish "high operational, development and environmental standards" (King County Code 21.34.010).

51

TABLE IX

HOUSING CHARACTERISTICS*

SEA-TAC WESTSIDE VICINITY

CENSUS TRACT	TOTAL UNITS	VACANT UNITS	SUB-STANDARD	% OWNER OCCUPIED	MEDIAN VALUE	MEDIAN RENT	PERSONS/HOUSEHOLD OWN	RENT	ALL
280	1,072	110	4	45.8%	$22,900	$144	3.4	2.1	2.4
285	1,240	73	12	75.5%	$23,200	$135	3.7	2.5	3.4
TOTAL	2,312	7.9%	0.7%	62.1%					
KING COUNTY	423,183	7.4%	2.8%	63.2%	$20,000	$117			2.9

*1970 Census Data

Environmental Impact

Construction of the proposed Headquarters building is not expected to have
measurable impact on population or housing in the site vicinity or to cause
any significant shift in population within the region. The new facility will
replace current headquarters operations in south Seattle, approximately 6
miles to the north, and all of the 200 employees would be relocated from the
Seattle facility. Few, if any, employees are expected to change their resi-
dence location because of the move.

As discussed in the "Land Use" section of this report, the proposal should
have no adverse impact on housing or population in the site vicinity. The
most significant potential impact would be the stabilizing effect of providing a definite physical barrier to further westward expansion of the airport,
which would remove much of the present uncertainty about the future of existing residential land uses in the vicinity.

TRANSPORTATION AND CIRCULATION

Existing Conditions

The region and the project vicinity are well served by transportational facilities. Seattle is a major international seaport. The site is readily accessible
to Sea-Tac International Airport and to Boeing Field as well. Seattle is
also located on the main lines of the Burlington Northern, Union Pacific, and
Milwaukee Road railroads.

Access to the site itself would be provided by the local highway and street
system. The project vicinity is well served by freeways and major arterials
in north-south and east-west directions.

60

184

North-south arterials with their approximate average daily traffic loads
include:[*]

1) Interstate 5, freeway, approximately 70,000 ADT.
2) Pacific Highway South, 21,000 ADT.
3) SR 509, freeway, 24,000 ADT at intersection with SR 518.
4) Des Moines Way, 7,500 ADT north of intersection with South
156th Street.

East-west arterials with their approximate average daily traffic loads include:

1) SR 518, freeway, 37,000 ADT.
2) South 154th Street, secondary arterial, 6,000 ADT north
of proposed site.
3) South 188th Street, major arterial, 15,000 ADT south of
proposed site.

The site is now accessible via 12th Avenue South which parallels the west
boundary of the site, and by Port of Seattle roads inside of the security
fence for Sea-Tac Airport. Twelfth Avenue South is classified in the King County
Interim Transportation Plan as a local access street. As such, it is intended
to provide vehicular and pedestrian access only to and among the adjacent
single-family residences. The local residents have voiced strong opposition
to any increase in traffic along 12th Avenue South. The adopted Highline
Communities Plan proposes a 12th Avenue South street project that would include bicycle and pedestrian facilities, landscaping and drainage improvements. The proposed access roads were located to avoid any increase in traffic
along 12th Avenue South.

South 154th Street between 12th Avenue South and 24th Avenue South has a 2 lane,
20 foot wide cement concrete pavement which appears to be in good condition.
The roadway has a 10 foot wide gravel shoulder along the north side and a 6 foot
wide bladed shoulder along the south side. The right-of-way is 60 feet wide and
the roadway is posted with a 35 mph speed limit. A signed and marked school
crosswalk exists across the west leg of the intersection of South 156th Way
and 12th Avenue South.

[*] County Road Traffic counts were supplied by the King County Traffic and
Planning Division. Traffic counts for State Highways were obtained from
the Washington State Highway Department.

61

The traffic-carrying capacity of the South 154th Street - South 156th Way roadway is approximately 550 vehicles per hour in one direction, computed for level of service "C". Level of service "C", on the 1965 Highway Capacity Manual's scale from A to F, is the level of service commonly used for the design of roadways in urban and suburban areas. The 1990 average peak hour volume for this roadway is projected to be approximately 340 vehicles in one direction. South 154th Street is scheduled by the county for minor widening and reconstruction with construction to begin by 1980.

The present METRO transit bus system would not provide convenient transportation for the site.

Environmental Impact

The estimated trips that would be generated by the proposed facility are pre-sented in the following table. The table and assessment of traffic impacts were developed by a consulting traffic engineer for the project sponsor.

TABLE X *

BOEING CORPORATE HEADQUARTERS

Assumed Vehicular Trip Distribution Over Time
Average Work Day for Initial Employment Situation

Hour Ending	Vehicular Trips			
	Employee	Delivery	Visitor & Misc.	Total
8:00 AM	180	3	7	190
9:00 AM	30	3	27	60
10:00 AM	30	3	27	60
11:00 AM	30	3	27	60
12:00 Noon	30	3	27	60
1:00 PM	90	3	17	110
2:00 PM	30	3	27	60
3:00 PM	30	3	27	60
4:00 PM	30	3	27	60
5:00 PM	170	3	7	180
	650	30	220	900

* Transportation Planning & Engineering, Inc.

62

186

Short-Term Environmental Uses vs. Long-Term Productivity

Construction activity related to the project would last approximately two years. The facility's ultimate life would exceed fifty years.

The site and the north buffer zone encompassing the proposed north access road would be committed to the proposed uses for the foreseeable future. The proposed facility would define the future of land use along this portion of the western boundary of Sea-Tac Airport for the foreseeable future.

Development of the site would increase revenues to the Port of Seattle and taxes to both local and state agencies. While commitment of the site in accordance with the proposal would preclude development of a purely passive buffer, it would also preclude possible future development of the site for airport related facilities. While the proposed facility would limit future airport related development options for the Port of Seattle, it would remove uncertainty about future use of this site and much of the western airport boundary and thus, could have a stabilizing effect on the westside communities.

The land is not a significant natural area or unusual recreational resource. The proposed facility would not significantly affect the long-term productivity of the site as a natural area or recreational resource.

72

Alternatives to the Proposal

No-Action

Denial of the proposed plan amendments and rezone requests would direct the project sponsor to an alternative site. The proposed site would remain as undeveloped open space. Although funding is not currently available, the viewpoint park would presumably be developed by the Port of Seattle in the next few years. The buffer area along 12th Avenue South would be landscaped. This could also be viewed by some as having a positive reinforcing impact on the west side residential areas.

Since the demand for various aviation related facilities will continue to increase it is possible that there would be proposals in the future to develop the site for such facilities if the present proposal is not approved.

Current policies and plans offer a measure of protection to the open-space, buffer zone along the western boundary of Sea-Tac. With changing political circumstances and increasing demand for aviation related facilities, the protecting policies and plans may become subject to change. Therefore, while the immediate no-action alternative is to retain the open space and develop the viewpoint, the long-term result may be indefinite.

Alternative Sites

After an initial consideration of over 20 potential sites, the project sponsor narrowed the field to five sites for further consideration. These included three sites adjacent to existing major airports, a suburban site in the Sea-Tac vicinity and a site adjacent to an existing Boeing plant.

Considerations in selecting a site included architectural potential, corporate identity, site expansion capability, community acceptance, zoning compatibility, traffic impact, air quality sensitivity, utility availability and soil conditions The west side of Sea-Tac was selected as the most favorable site considering all factors. Many of the environmental impacts associated with the project would be similar for all sites. The primary factors in selecting the Sea-Tac site were architectural potential, corporate identity with aircraft and expansion potential. A summary of the sponsor's comparative analysis used in site selection is shown in Figure 16.

74

188

APPENDIX A

COMMENTS AND RESPONSES TO THE DRAFT EIS

This Appendix contains letters of comment from agencies, individuals and private organizations to the Draft EIS for the
Boeing Corporate Headquarters facility.

The letters are reproduced in full and where a response is
appropriate it is given on a following page.

King County and the Port of Seattle wish to express their
appreciation to all commenting agencies and citizens for the
time and effort spent in reviewing the Draft EIS.

CONTENTS OF APPENDIX A

A-1

189

PSCOG Grand Central on the Park • 216 First Avenue South • Seattle, Wash. 98104 • 206/464-7090

Puget Sound Council of Governments

January 27, 1978

RECEIVED
FEB 6 1978
DEPARTMENT OF PLANNING
& COMMUNITY DEVELOPMENT

John P. Lynch, Director
Department of Planning and Community Development
W 313 King County Courthouse
516 Third Avenue
Seattle WA 98104

Dear Mr. Lynch:

The King County Subregional Council acting through the Growth
and Development Committee has reviewed the Draft Environmental
Impact Statement for the proposed Boeing Headquarters at Sea-Tac
Airport for which the Department of Planning and Community
Development is the lead agency.

The Committee reviewed the DEIS against the adopted Goals and
Policies for Regional Development and identified those policies
which support the project and those which are in conflict with
the project. In each instance where the project was identified
as in conflict with an adopted policy the Committee discussed
the matter and has concurred in the attached comments and
questions.

The Committee was generally supportive of the project as a
suitable use for the green belt/buffer strip along the westside
of the airport. The review which is attached did raise a couple
of questions that we hope can be answered in the FEIS.

It is the hope of the Subregional Council and the Committee on
Growth and Development that the factors identified in our review
will be useful to you and to other King County officials in
reaching decisions on the projects and in identifying mitigation
measures where necessary.

Respectfully,

Councilmember Paul Kraabel, Chairman
Committee on Growth and Development
King Subregional Council

A-10

King Subregional Council • 666 Bellevue Way S.E. • Bellevue, Washington 98009 • 206/455-7669

DRAFT ENVIRONMENTAL IMPACT STATEMENT REVIEW

TITLE: The Boeing Company Corporate Headquarters Facility

LEAD AGENCY: King County Department of Community Development

Project Supports the Following
GPRD Policies

Activity Centers   -   Policy #2
Policy #2 - New economic activities
should be encouraged as a first
order of preference to locate in
existing centers, and as a second
order preference to group into
new centers, rather than locate
in dispersed, stripped or
isolated areas.

Agriculture   - none identified
Economic   - none identified
Housing   - none identified
Natural Environment- none identified
Public Services - none identified
Transportation   - none identified

Intergovernmental Relations - none
                             identified

Fiscal   - none identified
Social   - none identified

Project Conflicts with the
Following GPRD Policies

Activity Centers - none identified

Agriculture - none identified
Economic   - none identified
Housing   - none identified
Natural Environment - none identified
Public Services - none identified

Transportation   - Policy #11
Encourage a careful assessment of
transportation investments that
may further increase the efficiency
of present transportation facilities
and services, taking account of
energy, environment, community
and fiscal implications.

Intergovernmental Relations - none
                             identified

Fiscal -none identified

Social - none identified

Identified GPRD Policies

Activity Centers - Policy #2 - Although PSCOG
has not yet identified any activity centers
in King County, it is recognized that Sea-Tac
Airport is the focus of a growing range of
economic activities. The Boeing Headquarters
appears to be consistent in the broad sense of
this policy but the EIS should provide
additional detail about the choice of the
residentially oriented west side for the site.
Are there other sites in the vicinity of the
airport that could be used for the Boeing
Headquarters? Is a view of the airport the most
important consideration?

Transportation - Policy #11 - The Boeing
Headquarters is not a transportation facility
but it does affect the public investment in
Sea-Tac Airport to the degree that it limits
future airport expansion. The EIS should
present a more detailed discussion of the
implications of limiting airport expansion for
the future.

A-11

191

January 24, 1978

WESTSIDE HILLTOP RESIDENTIAL AREA
Response to Draft EIS
The Boeing Company Corporate Headquarters Facility

We, the homeowners and residents of the Westside Hilltop residential community, fully recognize the dynamic nature of the Sea-Tac Airport as a regional air terminal. We are, therefore, not opposed to an orderly, well-planned and compatible future airport westside development as long as our community has guaranteed safeguards. We are all reasonable people trying to maintain a viable residential community.

The Sea-Tac Communities Plan (STCP), adopted by both the Port of Seattle and King County Council, redesignated the hilltop community as a Residential Reinforcement area and limited westside airport development to south of South 176th street. On April 4, 1977, the County Council passed motion #02957 which reaffirmed this requirement for land use compatibility by stating "...airport facility development on the west side of the Sea-Tac Airport should be limited to the area south of South 176th...". On December 19, 1977, the County Council adopted the Highline Communities Plan (HCP) which designates "airport facility" on the west side of the airport south of South 176th Street only, and designates a combination of "airport open Space" and "parks and recreation" north of 176th up to South 156th Way.

The proposed 25 acre office complex will require a rezoning to manufacturing park which seems to be contrary to the philosophy of residential reinforcement. A reversal in land use from that designated in the STCP will have a significant impact on our community unless positive measures are taken to protect it. We earnestly hope that the County Council will take positive steps to implement measures to reinforce our residential reinforcement status. As an example, in the fall of 1977, the County Council denied rezoning to Airport Open Use (AOU) of the Marchell property, which is immediately north of the site now being asked for rezoning by the Port. This reclassification to AOU was denied by reason of land use incompatibility. A review of county ordinance #3148, passed the 11th of April, 1977, represents or defines AOU as a more compatible land use than the manufacturing park zoning now being requested by the Port.

We do not want a Georgetown developing in our Hilltop area. We had a residential neighborhood that used to be better than it is now. We had a community with normal community ammenities.

We cannot accept, therefore, any further development north of South 176th Street until the Port, in cooperation with the community and King County, carefully evaluates the extent of potential westside development, and devises and implements measures which will:

    A. Protect our property values;

    B. Protect the quality of our life;

    C. Protect our community's attractiveness and viability.

Luella Gestner, Secretary
Westside Hilltop Survival Committee

Received by Planning Svc 1/24/78 at Public Meet

A-26

SUMMARY

PUBLIC MEETING ON THE DRAFT EIS
BOEING CORPORATE HEADQUARTERS FACILITY

January 24, 1978
7:00 p.m., Highline High School Cafetorium

Thirty-eight persons were in attendance; sixteen of those were
agency, Boeing, consultant and press representatives. The meeting
was tape recorded.

WELCOMING COMMENTS

Barbara Summers, Sea-Tac PAC member and "Hilltop" resident:High-
lighted three key issues facing her neighborhood; 1) SR509 extension;
2) proposed Weyerhauser aviation facility and 3) proposed Boeing
office. Cited a Hilltop area survey which indicated 70% not opposed
to Boeing headquarters, with Safeguards; not opposed, 30%; opposed,
28%; 6% , no opinion.

Dottie Harper, Highline Community Council representative:Welcomed
attendees, expressed the Council's interest in community facilities
and invited public comment on the Draft EIS.

INTRODUCTION

Harold Robertson, King County Planning Division: The Boeing
request is for a comprehensive plan revision and a zoning reclassification. The review process began with the filing of a request
for rezone from RS7200 to M-P and issuance of the Draft EIS.

The public hearing before the King County Zoning and Subdivision
Hearing Examiner will be March 23. The County Council will make
the final decision on the requested plan change and rezone. After
Council action, the Port of Seattle Commission will take action on
the plan change request.

Availability of Draft EIS on Weyerhauser proposal was mentioned.

The deadlines for comment on both the Weyerhauser and Boeing EIS's
were announced.(January 28 and February 6, respectively.)

SUMMARY DESCRIPTION OF ENVIRONMENTAL IMPACTS

Ron Ubaghs. of Wilsey and Ham, consultants: Reviewed the impacts
described in the Draft EIS regarding topography, drainage,
vegetation, air quality, noise, light and glare, land use, traffic,

A-51

public services, utilities and aesthetics.

It was stated that there would be 30-40 vehicles per hour, during peak hour (8:15 - 9:15 a.m.).

A question was raised regarding helicopter flights. That noise impact was discussed.

COMMENT AND DISCUSSION

1. Raymond Vye, 16043 12th Ave. So.: Felt there was a possibility that the number of helicopter flights would be increased.

2. Louella Gesner, Secretary, Hilltop Survival Committee:
    Read a response to the Draft EIS from the Committee, highlighting 1) a desire for guaranteed safeguards for a viable residential community; 2) the history of the residential reinforcement desig- nation, including Council Motion 02957 and the Highline Communi- ties Plan; 3) a need for implementation of measures to guarantee residential reinforcement. The Committee cannot accept develop- ment north of S. 176th St., until the Port and Council will protect property values and protect quality of life.

3. Alice Wetzel, 578 S. 158th Street:
    Zoning - read the stated purposes of both the RM-900 and M-P zones. Permitted uses and restrictions were also cited. Sees M-P zoning as "a foot in the door" to establish an industrial area on Sea-Tac's west side. RM-900 with a P-Suffix could be used, M-P is not required. The proposal is totally unacceptable if M-P zoning goes with it.

    Landscaping - EIS does not mention the Scout tree planting project. Who is to do the landscaping for the Boeing project?

    View Point Park - Proposal would reduce it to 1/4 of the original land area.

    The Westside Residential Community (lowlands) is not adequately addressed in the EIS.

    Proposed an alternative: 1) leave the existing view point park; 2) restore the old Evergreen tennis courts; 3) move the Boeing project to the south of the existing viewpoint area and move general aviation facilities to the south of S. 176th St.

A-52

4. Raymond Vye: Discussed Scout involvement.

5. Chris Hansen, 16416 2nd S.W.
   Questions M-P zoning classification and asked about the staff
   recommendation. The response was that Boeing was advised
   that M-P was the appropriate classification to request, in
   that manufacturing or office park described the proposal more
   accurately than maximum density residential and RM-900 may
   be misleading on the zoning map. It was pointed out that
   no staff recommendation has yet been made - the final EIS is
   necessary before development of a staff report for the
   rezone hearing.

6. Pauline Conradi, 16053 12th So.:
   The access roads (pages 16 and 20) appear to allow north-
   south through traffic. Will the road remain in Port hands?
   Who will maintain it? Cited earlier position paper which
   stated that additional traffic should be diverted to perimeter
   road to the east, not to S. 156th Way. Reasons noted were
   existing traffic, the proposed athletic field complex,
   congestion and safety hazards. Expressed concern about the
   impact of auto trips to the south of the site. There should
   be a link to the SR509 extension.

   The EIS has not addressed the protection of property values.
   The proposals suggested in the position paper are not addressed
   in the EIS.

   It is incorrect to conclude that the Boeing project will
   alleviate neighborhood uncertainties.

7. Virginia Dana, 2648 S. 142nd St.
   Read a statement. Boeing could be a large plus to the
   community. The Boeing location will fix that section of the
   west airport boundary and will relieve some uncertainties.

   Traffic and construction impacts noted.

   Airport vicinity residents always have a somewhat unforseeable
   future.

   The State of Washington needs an extra push to require noise
   remedies and to help fund them.

8. Marian MacKenzie, 21230 15th Ave. So.
   Invited Boeing to locate their office in her neighborhood.

A-53

9. Carol Burwald, 1010 S. 174th.:
   The three key projects impacting her area: 1) the General/
   Corporate avaiation proposal; 2) the Boeing proposal and
   3) SR509 extension.

   Her area is surrounded by negative noise impacts. When
   you add all plane and auto traffic together, there will be
   significant air quality impacts. Should be protected against
   property devaluation.

10. Mike Colasurdo, 1129 S.W. 121st Pl.:
    Boeing proposal is a wonderful thing for the community.
    However, other proprerties around Sea-Tac, under private
    ownership and zoned for manufacturing should be used.

11. Barbara Summers, 1016 S. 174th St.:
    Opposes Boeing and Weyerhauser proposals because she moved
    into a residential area. Now it is proposed for office
    buildings and an aircraft center. That's not what they moved
    there for.

12. Questions and discussion followed here regarding site
    selection (why here?), helicopter flights (extent of impact),
    traffic flow on S. 156th Way (what is the directional split,
    based on the location of employee homes?), M-P zoning
    (what will it draw, or attract?), experience in other areas
    (what do corporate headquarters and general/corporate aviation
    headquarters attract? Would they serve as a drawing card to
    other uses?)

13. Don Davis, Boeing Company, 8457 NE 7th, Bellevue:
    For the 30 acres which is the subject of the Boeing proposal,
    there are no plans or intentions for industrial facilities.
    As for the buffer area to the north, Boeing cannot negotiate
    with the Port on specifics (e.g., the road) until the final
    EIS is issued.

14. Paul Barden, King County Councilman:
    Port Commissioner Simonsen informed him that no use of the
    buffer area to the north is contemplated.

15. Howard Kehrer, "lowlands":
    Concerned about deterioration of the neighborhood.

    Meeting concluded, followed by informal discussion and
    examination of maps and models.

HR:eg
1/27/78

A-54

INDEX

ABOUT THE AUTHOR

CAROLYN J. LOGAN, a reporter since 1974, has covered county government for three years, including for the Walla Walla Union-Bulletin, a Washington daily. Formerly with the Lewiston Morning Tribune, she now reports for the Highline Times, near Seattle. Her work on property issues has appeared in The Christian Science Monitor. She has firsthand experience in real estate, particularly in development. Her background includes coordinating the Coalition for Open Government, which formed the nucleus for successful Initiative 276 campaign. Establishment of the Washington Public Disclosure Commission resulted from the campaign.